HENCHGIRL™

WORTH IT!
DONT GIVE UP
JORNEL
HOW TO STOP READING SELF-HELP BOOKS

HENCHGIRL™

KRISTEN GUDSNUK

President & Publisher MIKE RICHARDSON
Editor SHANTEL LaROCQUE
Designer BRENNAN THOME
Digital Art Technician MELISSA MARTIN

Published by Dark Horse Books
A division of Dark Horse Comics, Inc.
10956 SE Main Street
Milwaukie, OR 97222

DarkHorse.com
KristenGudsnuk.com

First edition: March 2017
ISBN 978-1-50670-144-8

10 9 8 7 6 5 4 3 2
Printed in Canada

To find a comics shop in your area, call the Comic Shop Locator Service toll-free at 1-888-266-4226.
International Licensing: (503) 905-2377

Henchgirl was originally published online at HenchgirlComic.com and in single issues by Scout Comics.

Names: Gudsnuk, Kristen, author, illustrator.
Title: Henchgirl / by Kristen Gudsnuk.
Description: First edition. | Milwaukie, OR : Dark Horse Books, 2017. | "Henchgirl was originally published online at HenchgirlComic.com and in single issues by Scout Comics"
Identifiers: LCCN 2016050458 | ISBN 9781506701448 (paperback)
Subjects: LCSH: Graphic novels. | BISAC: COMICS & GRAPHIC NOVELS / Superheroes. | COMICS & GRAPHIC NOVELS / Crime & Mystery.
Classification: LCC PN6727.G766 H46 2017 | DDC 741.5/973--dc23
LC record available at https://lccn.loc.gov/2016050458

HENCHGIRL

BY
KRISTEN GUDSNUK

KRISTEN GUDSNUK

ISSUE 1

LOOKS LIKE YOU'VE FLOWN INTO MY TRAP, MR. GREAT GUY!

AHHH!

SUE: were go
watching the n
scary thing 4
?!!!!
ME: I told you
to wait for meee
:(((((((((((((

RING RING RING
SURRENDER, FIEND!
NO THANKS.

YOU WON'T GET AWAY, MONSIEUR BUTTERFLY!

AGHH

W-WON'T I?
FWOO

NOT WITHOUT YOUR RIDE!
FWOOOO
THE BUTTERFLY BUGGIE!!
SHUUU
...
!!
Heh.
BOOM!!

Wee ooo wee ooo
THESE MEAN STREETS.
nghh...

where did she go?
FWOOSH
THESE MEAN, MEAN STREETS.

THEY CHEW YOU UP AND THEY SPIT YOU OUT.
honk
THAT'S ROADMEISTER. JUST ANOTHER VILLAIN IN CREPE CITY.

AS FOR ME...
AHHHH!
LURCH!

HOBBLE

wee ooo wee ooo

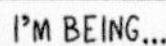
I'M BEING...
CARRIED?

WHO IS HE?
YOU NEED TO GO TO THE HOSPITAL.
I'LL... I'LL GIVE YOU **20 BUCKS**... IF YOU TAKE ME **HOME**...
UH...

OH, LIKE, **MY** PLACE. YOU KNOW. TEEHEE.

WHERE DO YOU LIVE?

98 MONARCH AVE...
'N' MAKE IT SNAPPY.

I CAN SEE... UP HIS NOSE.
THIS MYSTERIOUS... **"HUMAN TAXI."**
Out of business
Storage

98

HERE'S YOUR FARE, **HUMAN TAXI.**

THAT'S... NOT MY NAME. AND I'M NOT IN IT FOR THE **MONEY**.

...
stuff

I'M HOME
AHHHH!
28
creeoak

WOO! SCARY THING 4!
YOU REALLY NEED **HEALTH INSURANCE.**

BANK
OPEN
ENE
CRIME SCENE
CR

PARDON OUR APPEARANCE

NEXT!

...
Uh...hi.
FRED

I'D LIKE TO MAKE A DEPOSIT.

FRED

WHAT'S GOING ON HERE? **RENOVATING?**
WE GOT HIT BY THE **BUTTERFLY GANG** LAST NIGHT.

I'M SURPRISED YOU DIDN'T HEAR ABOUT IT.

Oh, that's TERRIBLE!
JUST... SIGN THE PAD.

YOUR DEPOSIT IS COMPLETE.
Bank Poster

That wasn't very polite, Fred.
....
I'M RICH!

STO AGE
SPACE FOR RENT CALL 718-STOAGE
SIGH...

WHEN ARE THESE **DAMN COMMIES** GONNA GET HERE? IT'S BEEN **45 MINUTES** ALREADY!
EXORCISE: The key to a happy afterlife?
BUTTERFLY

GOT SOMEWHERE TO BE, LARRY?

IT'S MY DAUGHTER'S DAMN **BIRTHDAY.**
BUTTERFLY

OH **NO**! WHY AREN'T YOU **WITH** HER?
I NEED THE MONEY FROM THIS GIG TO GET THE POOR KID A DECENT **CAKE** AND A **BARBIE.**

SHE'S WAITIN' AT HOME FOR **DADDY...**

LARRY. GO TO HER. **PLEASE.** TAKE THIS.

YOU SURE YOU CAN HANDLE THE **MOLOTOVS** ALL BY **YOURSELF?**
OH YEAH. YOU JUST GIVE YOUR LITTLE GIRL A **HUG** FROM ME.

THANKS, MARY! I REALLY OWE YOU ONE!

12:16

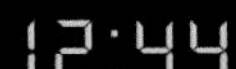
12:44

...

1:37

FLASH
FLASH

THIS ONE,
THIS ONE,
AND...

THIS ONE.

ZZIP

KHOROSHO.
IOU

THIS IS NOT **DISCREET.**
NOT, HOW SHOULD I SAY...
PRACTICAL.
GLITTER GIRL

WE HAVE TO KEEP THE **MOTIF** GOING OR THE BOSS GETS MAD.
I UNDERSTAND.
MR. MOLOTOV COCKTAIL

NO PARKING
UGH... IT'S SO LATE...

MEANWHILE...
STOP RIGHT THERE!

WHO'S **THIS** CLOWN?
YOU DA **NUTCRACKER** OR SOMETHIN'?

WHAT? NO, I'M...

MANNEQUIN.
I'VE HAD **ENOUGH** OF THIS WACKO.

HA HA HA

STOP RIGHT THERE!!

...

BUTTERFLY...

ZAP!

squish
HEY, HEY, I CAN WALK!

OH, THE PRIDE OF MAN.
dust

WELL, I GUESS WE'RE ...

EVEN?
FWIP

OH WELL!
shrug!
LASER EMPORIUM
GIVE A CREPE
Keep Crepe City Beautiful

YAWN!

SUE! YOU'RE UP?
IT'S 7. NORMAL-PEOPLE HOURS.

I'M SO WIPED. GIMME SOME CEREAL. CAN YOU UNHOOK MY GIRDLE?

FLOOP

I SET UP A JOB INTERVIEW FOR YOU. FOR AN HONEST JOB. YOU CAN EVEN PAY TAXES.
PFFF!

HERE'S THE INFO.
WHAAAT?! TAXES? THANK YOU!

GOOD LUCK! PLEASE TRY TO GET THIS.
SCRATCH MY BACK...

DON'T YOU WANT...
...YOUR CEREAL?

UH... YOU CAN FINISH IT.

PERFECT!

HAIR STUFF

JUST FIVE MINUTES...

IT'S JOB TIME.

TOTAL E-CLIPS of the HAIR
TURN AROUND BALLET STUDIO
BRIGHT EYES
CREPELBEE'S
SO, MS. POSA. WHAT HAVE YOU BEEN DOING THE PAST FEW YEARS?

YOUR RÉSUMÉ JUST SAYS "????????".
CRAP... DID I PRINT THE WRONG *FILE?*
WELL, I'VE JUST BEEN WORKING ODD JOBS.
MARY POSA
???????
went to skool
I need a job plz
hi mom

BABYSITTING. ***MODELING.*** INVESTING. I MADE A SHORT FILM...

WOW! I'M SOMETHING OF AN AMATEUR INVESTOR MYSELF! WHAT'S YOUR PORTFOLIO STRATEGY?
...

...

Ms. Posa?

ARE YOU ASLEEP?!
NO!!

Sigh...

HAVE YOU EVER BEEN CONVICTED OF A CRIME?
N-NOT *CONVICTED*, NO.
IS THERE A REASON YOU STRESSED THE WORD *"CONVICTED"*?

NO I DIDN'T!!

TELL ME WHY YOU'D BE A GOOD FIT AT *CREPELBEE'S.*
I JUST LOVE SERVING PEOPLE!

LIKE, A LOT!

IT GIVES ME A WARM, FUZZY FEELING.

I... I THINK I UNDERSTAND.

AND I'LL TAKE ANY SHIFTS! I NEVER SLEEP!
MARY POSA
?????
HIRE ME!!

WE'LL GET BACK TO YOU.

NAILED IT!
CREPEL
WHY NOT?
PULL

WORTH IT

ONE THING:
I CAN'T KNOW WHY...

IT REALLY DOESN'T MATTER HOW HARD YOU TRY.

UNLOCK YOUR POTENTIAL

YOU! BUT HAPPY

THE BUTTERFLY DEN
NO PARKING
KRR!

WELL, IT AIN'T WHAT I WOULDA GONE WITH...
IT'S...
DOES IT VIBRATE?
Ooh!

BEAUTIFUL!
'S BEAUTIFUL!

THE MONARCH SCEPTER!
BZZZ!

SEEMS TO BE IN WORKING ORDER.

NOW, EVERYONE, TAKE A SEAT.
OUR FIRST ORDER OF BUSINESS: EMPLOYEE OF THE WEEK!
WHO WILL GET TO WEAR THE WINGS THIS TIME?

WILL IT BE MARY POSA?

LARRY VA?
PALAWAN BIRDWING?
CHRIS SALIS?
Sigh...
KATIE PILLAR?

AND IT'S COCO OON! OUR LONGTIME REIGNING CHAMPION!
!!
COME ON UP HERE, COCO!

THANK YOU SO MUCH FOR THIS HONOR, MONSIEUR BUTTERFLY!

NOW, LET'S TALK SCHEMES. DOES ANYONE HAVE A DEVILISH PLAN TO RAVAGE CREPE CITY?

HAS ANYONE HEARD OF THE ST. CREPICIUS HOME FOR ORPHANS?

I GREW UP THERE. DO YOU KNOW SISTER ELIZABETH?

THE DIRECTOR AND I HAVE BEEN IN TALKS FOR A FEW WEEKS. HE'S OUR KIND OF GUY.
HE WAS RECENTLY GRANTED CITY FUNDING FOR RENOVATIONS, MORE BEDS, AND A NEW WING. YOU SEE...

THE ORPHANAGE IS **HAZARDOUSLY OVERCROWDED.** ORPHANS BEING TURNED AWAY **EVERY DAY.**

SORRY

St. Crepicius Home for TRAGIC ORPHANS
NO VACANCY
ORPHANS TURN BACK

ANYWAY, HE'LL SPLIT THE FUNDING MONEY WITH US. ALL WE HAVE TO DO IS EXERT A LITTLE **MUSCLE.**

BLOCK **CONSTRUCTION,** GET THE ZONING COMMISSION TO DECLARE THE SITE **DANGEROUS** FOR **WORKERS...** KEEPING THE WORK AT A PERPETUAL **STANDSTILL.**

HOW MUCH **DOUGH** ARE WE TALKING ABOUT?

MILLIONS.

EXCELLENT PLAN! THIS IS WHY YOU'RE MY **NUMBER ONE** FLY GIRL, COCO!

BUT...!

ALL THOSE LITTLE HOMELESS **ORPHANS...**
CLATTER!!

I TAKE IT YOU HAVE A **BETTER** IDEA?

grrrr!
WE BUILD THE WING OURSELVES!
MAYBE REACH OUT TO THE SALVATION ARMY FOR **MATTRESSES** AND STUFF...
Sigh..

FWOOSHHHH
EH?

WE COULD KEEP WHATEVER'S LEFT OVER FOR OURSELVES... IT'D BE A GOOD WORKOUT... BUILD TEAMWORK SKILLS...
UM... NO.

!!

THINK

WHAT IF WE ROB THE MUSEUM AGAIN?
WHAT WOULD WE STEAL?
umm...
ARTIFACTS?

REALLY CREATIVE, MARY. I GUESS WE'RE GOING WITH THE ORPHANAGE--

WHAT IF WE HIT...
GREG GAINS'S MANSION?

I'M LISTENING...

GAINS IS CREPE CITY'S WEALTHIEST BACHELOR. HE WOULDN'T MISS A FEW MILLION FROM HIS SECRET VAULT.
GREG GAINS
RICH GUY
AND HE'S ALWAYS HAVING THOSE BIG, FANCY PARTIES...

HIS NEXT PARTY IS SUPPOSED TO BE A MASKED BALL... "COME ONE, COME ALL" ...

GEE, I'D REALLY LOVE TO GO TO A BALL...

EXACTLY! GO IN LITTLE MASKS, HE WON'T KNOW WHAT HIT HIM!
AS LONG AS MY GRAND FOE MR. GREAT GUY DOESN'T MAKE AN APPEARANCE...

I LIKE IT! GREAT JOB, MARY!

HUH?!

WE'LL DO BOTH! NICE INITIATIVE, GIRLS!

HENCHGIRL
By Kristen Gudsnuk

KRISTEN GUDSNUK

Henchgirl

ISSUE 2

THE BALL

GAINS MANOR

LANA STREET, ACE REPORTER, HERE! AND WE'RE WATCHING **CREPE CITY'S ELITE** TRICKLING INTO THE *HOTTEST* **BACHELOR'S** BANQUET HALL! ALL IN **DISGUISE!**
"Hottest"?

OH, **LANA.** YOU'RE **DEFINITELY** INVITED.

THERE, YOU LOOK **GORGEOUS.**
I CAN'T PASS ON THIS OPPORTUNITY! BACK TO YOU, STAN!

REALLY?!

THESE TWO ARE **DEFINITELY** ON THE GUEST LIST.

SUCH A **RAVISHING** FIGURE, MADAME.

...CONSUELO, **HOW MANY** TIMES DO I HAVE TO TELL YOU TO USE THE **BACK** ENTRANCE?!
...LO SIENTO?

AWW, SHE THINKS SHE'S **PEOPLE**.

HAHAHAHAHA

ADIOS, CONSUELO. **ADIOS!**

ha ha ha

Servants' & Paupers' Entrance

CHP CHP CHP
I'M HERE TO HELP OUT. WHO'S **CONSUELO?**

I AM CONSUELO SUAREZ.

...WELL, AT LEAST HE MISTOOK ME FOR SOMEONE **ATTRACTIVE.**
BUT ABUELITA IS **ALSO** NAMED CONSUELO.

¿Qué?

Two Consuelos?
WE ARE NO SUPPOSED TO WEAR THE MASKS.

OH, GOOD.
I CAN HARDLY SEE IN THIS THING.

YOU!

DO I KNOW YOU?
N-NO.
taktaktaktak

ENCHANTÉE. I'M MARY.

I'M FRED.

I THINK YOU... COME TO MY **BANK** SOMETIMES.

YOU'VE GOT **TWO** JOBS? SAVE SOME FOR THE **REST** OF US!

AW YEAH
GOOD ONE

W-WE'RE RUNNING OUT OF **HORS D'OEUVRES!**

¡sí se puede!
GET TO WORK, TEAM!

SQULCH
SHK SHK SHK

hey! guys!
lol so true
mrmph
ha ha

Sigh...

grr
no fair

I'M GONNA HELP SERVE DRINKS.

WOULD YOU TWO LIKE ANY **REFRESHMENTS?**
CHAMPAGNE!

NO, IT'S **ME!** CAN WE GET ON WITH OUR **MISSION** HERE?

THIS PLACE IS TOTALLY **VULNERABLE** RIGHT NOW! LOOK AT THE **GUARDS!**

NO ENTRY

OHHH, MAYBE IN A BIT. ***HIC*** BUT FIRST, WE MUST HAVE MORE **CHAMPERS.**
MORE CHAMPAGNE!
UGH!!
STOMP STOMP

STOMP

STOMP
STOM

STOMP

STOMP

JEWELRY ROOM

FWIP FWIP

MARY.

W-WHAT?!
I GOT LOST.

I CAN'T LET YOU DO THIS.

WHY DO **YOU** CARE?

I **DON'T.** I JUST DON'T WANT THE **OTHER** WAIT STAFF TO GET **BLAMED** FOR THE **THEFT.**

I'M NOT A REAL EMPLOYEE.

I'M NOT EVEN GETTING **PAID** TO DO THIS! AND I WORKED SO **HARD**!

hic

H-HEY...

smoosh

THERE YOU GO.

I CAN TALK TO THE AGENCY I WORK FOR. GET YOU SIGNED UP.

REALLY?!

UMM... WELL, YOU NEED TO RETURN THAT JEWELRY.

THERE...

GOOD AS NEW.

NOW LET'S GET BACK TO THE KITCHEN.

YEAH!

CLATT

SERIOUSLY?

ADIOS!

TE QUIERO.

TAKE SOME COOKIES! **PLEASE!** YOU ARE TOO **SKINNY!**

YOU ARE **LITERALLY** MY FAVORITE PERSON, ABUELITA!
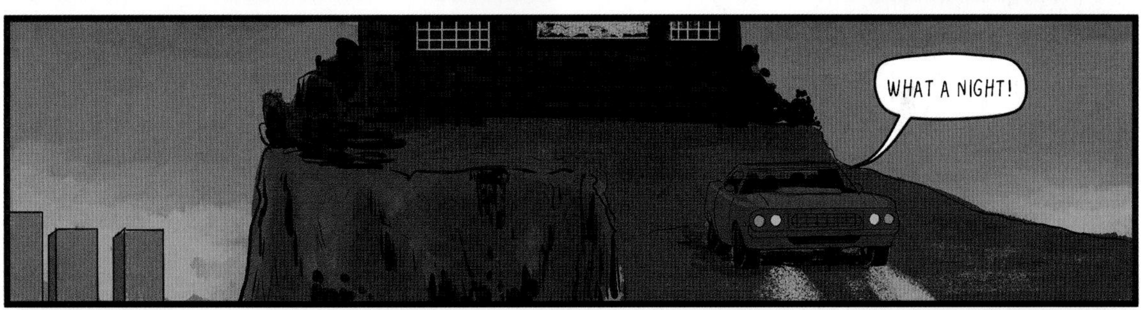
WHAT A NIGHT!

I HAD A **BLAST!**
ALTHOUGH IT DID GET A LITTLE WEIRD IN THE END.

LOOK AT THIS! **GIFT BAGS?!** A NEW **iDAD?!**
GOLD INGOTS! GIFT CARDS! LITTLE JARS OF CAVIAR!
iDAD
I'M VERY DISAPPOINTED IN YOU

AND GREGGIE GAVE ME THIS **ANTIQUE EMERALD NECKLACE!**

I GET TO KEEP THAT.

OH... OKAY.

YEAH, WELL, WE DIDN'T GET ANYTHING FOR THE **BUTTERFLY GANG.**

WE STILL HAVE THE **ORPHANS!**

...
YOUR MOTHER AND I ARE GETTING DIVORCED.

HEY! NEWS!
I AM NO LONGER THE BLACK SHEEP OF THE APARTMENT!

DID YOU KILL SOMEONE?
NO . . .

HAR, HAR.

ANYWAY, AS OF NOW I'VE GOT A REAL JOB! I'M A CATERER!

YOU QUIT THE BUTTERFLY GANG?

NOT YET, BUT . . . MAYBE SOMETIME SOON!

SO NOW YOU'VE GOT A SECRET IDENTITY!

CATERER BY DAY . . .

WORLD-CLASS CRIMINAL BY NIGHT . . .

I HAD AN IDENTITY ALREADY! I'M A PERSON, YOU KNOW!
NO YOU DIDN'T.
NOT REALLY.

NOW I GET TO PAY TAXES AND BE LIKE A REAL GROWNUP!
SO EXCITING!

TAXES ARE NOT FUN.

LET'S NOT BURST HER BUBBLE.

WELCOME VETS
annual dinner
STATE CHAMPS '89
CREPE LEAGUERS
P.S. 189
HOME
GUE
MORE GRAVY, SIR?
Next

YOU KNOW, YOU'RE NOT HALF-BAD AT CATERING.

REALLY ?!

WHAT ELSE AM I GOOD AT?

HEY!!
FORGET I SAID ANYTHING...

NOW THAT'S A NICE PIECE OF ASS!
I STILL GOT IT!

POTATOES
POTATOES

MORE APPLE JUICE?

GREAT TEAM EFFORT, EVERYONE!
HERE'S YOUR PAYCHECKS.
SCUZN

IS THIS THING MISSING A *ZERO?*

CATERA
PAY TO THE ORDER OF MARY POSA
510
ONE HUNDRED DOLLARS
$100
WORK

I DON'T KNOW WHAT KIND OF CATERING JOBS ***YOU'RE*** USED TO.
sorry...

WOW! SUCH FUN!
I ALMOST FORGOT ABOUT MY LIFE OF CRIME ***COMPLETELY!!***
PS184
BEEP!

crepizon 4:31
MESSAGES COCO EDIT
Hey gang <3 coco here. Larry, Chris, and Palawan, need u for St. Crepicius gig tonite. Free pizza/everyone gets a cut of earnings! <3

pizzaa...

SAVE US...
YOU DID THIS TO US..

WHY ARE YOU CRYING?
DID YOU GET FROSTING IN YOUR EYE AGAIN?
boo hoo hoo
poke

IF I TOLD YOU, I'D HAVE TO REVEAL ...

... THAT I KNOW YOUR SECRET IDENTITY.

I HAVE NO IDEA WHAT YOU'RE TALKING ABOUT.

ok bye Mary

AHA!

... MANNEQUIN.

OKAY, I GET IT!

YOUR DISGUISE IS PRETTY FLIMSY, FRED.

AS IS MINE.

I knew that.

ANYWAY . . .

I NEED YOUR HELP.

POST NO BILLS
CNN
DELI

HERE ARE THOSE EMAILS I PRINTED OUT.

GOOD LUCK.

RELAX. WHAT'S THE **WORST** THAT COULD HAPPEN?
CNN
CREPE NEWS NETWORK
...

THANKS FOR DOING THIS FOR ME...
FOR HIRE
THE END IS NIGH
CITY BEAU
CHAINSAW GANG

CREPE NEWS
YOU MEAN...
FOR THE **ORPHANS.**
"SCREECH"
THE PILLAGE VOICE
Lock up your valuables
FREE

ENCHGIRL

KRISTEN GUDSNUK

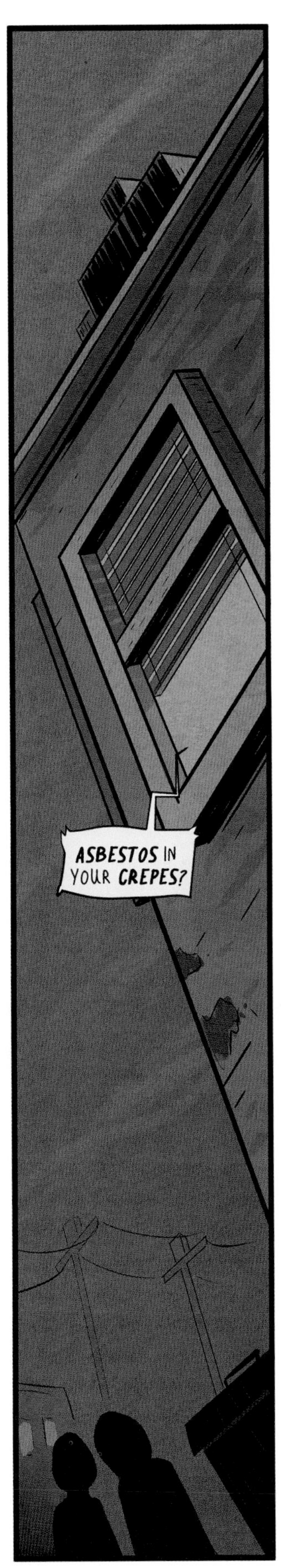
ASBESTOS IN YOUR CREPES?

SOUNDS PRETTY GROSS, BUT WHADDAYA KNOW, IT'S TRUE!
TONIGHT at 11
CNN

BREAKING NEWS!

LANA STREET
Ace Reporter

THE MAN IN CHARGE OF CREPE CITY'S MOST DERELICT ORPHANAGE—

ACCUSED OF POCKETING FEDERAL GRANT MONEY?

Crepizon 11:43 15%
BACK COCO
MANNEQUIN, alias Fred Stumbley, is the man responsible for leaking details of St. Crepicius plan. Anyone who finds him and brings him to the Butterfly Den will be rewarded $100,000.
...

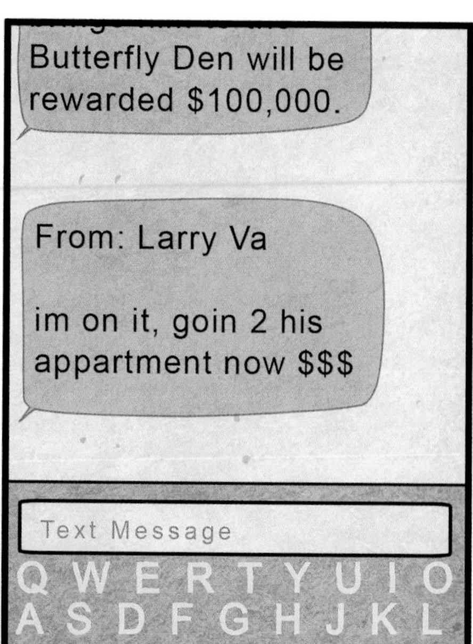
Butterfly Den will be rewarded $100,000.
From: Larry Va
im on it, goin 2 his appartment now $$$
Text Message
Q W E R T Y U I O
A S D F G H J K L

PUPPIES

FRED!
YOU'VE GOT TO COME HERE. YOU'RE NOT SAFE!

NO! RIGHT NOW!
FOR SERIOUS!

CALL ME WHEN YOU'RE HERE!

...
what?
...

whaaat?
WILSON
New SHOOZ
they're cool shoes

YOU'VE GOT TO HIDE OUT **HERE.** THEY KNOW YOU LEAKED THE ***INFORMATION!***

WAIT, THIS ***RANDOM GUY*** IS SLEEPING OVER?
I AM?

OH, PERFECT!
I MADE ***CARROT CAKE!***

YUM!
OOH!

LEMME GET THIS STRAIGHT: ***YOU TWO*** LEAKED THE ORPHANAGE SCANDAL?
YEP!

SUCH AN ***EXCITING*** LIFE OF CRIME . . .

I DON'T WANT TO IMPOSE ON YOUR HOSPITALITY...
DON'T WORRY...
I'M ACTUALLY KIND OF IMPRESSED!
OH, PSHAW!

MARY'S **ALWAYS** BRINGING GUYS TO SLEEP OVER!

OH, TINA, YOU AND YOUR **INDECIPHERABLE** SENSE OF HUMOR!
MRPH!

I GET THE BATHROOM FROM **7 TO 7:30**, AND TINA GETS IT FROM **7:30 TO 8**.
THAT IS OUR RULE.

LISTEN, I SHOULDN'T STAY HERE.
WHY DON'T I JUST GO TO THE **POLICE?** MAYBE THEY CAN GRANT ME ASYLUM. **WITNESS PROTECTION** AND ALL THAT.

THAT WON'T WORK. WE HAVE LIKE **THREE MOLES** THERE. THEY'LL GET YOU.
YOU SHOULD GET THEM **CHECKED OUT**. COULD BE **MELANOMA**...

GUYS, FRED DOESN'T HAVE ANY **POWERS**. WE HAVE TO HIDE HIM **HERE**.

I DO SO HAVE POWERS.

HUH?!
MY POWER IS THAT I CAN LEAVE MY BODY.
AND... AND THEN WHAT?!

SADLY WATCH MY BODY GET PUMMELED.

LIKE SO.

FW

FWOOOOOO

SOUNDS HOLLOW.
NOK NOK

NOK
um.

S-SORRY.
...?

BASICALLY, I CAN, LIKE, **ASTRAL PROJECT.** IT'S GOOD FOR SPYING.
UNFORTUNATELY, IF THE MANNEQUIN IS DAMAGED, I BECOME GRAVELY INJURED.
SO DON'T **EVER** TOUCH ME WHILE I'M A MANNEQUIN. MY **ARMS** COULD **FALL OFF.**
WILSON

NO FAIR, YOU HAVE **POWERS?!**
UH... YES.
PUPPIES

I DON'T HAVE POWERS. I MEAN, I HAVE ABNORMALLY SHARP **ELBOWS**, BUT I DON'T THINK THAT QUALIFIES.

HEY, YOU'RE PRETTY STRONG. I COULD NEVER HAVE CARRIED THAT **BOOKSHELF** INTO THE APARTMENT LIKE YOU DID...

I think you're supposed to take the books out first...

AWW, THANKS.
I HAVE POWERS, **TOO!**
PUPPIES

I CAN MAKE CARROTS APPEAR!

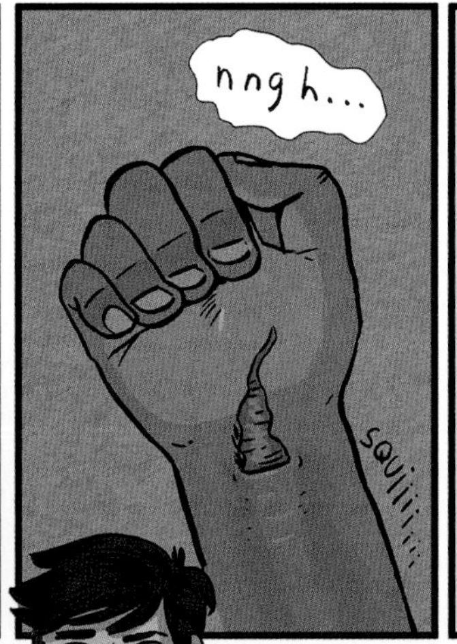
nngh...
SQUIIIIII

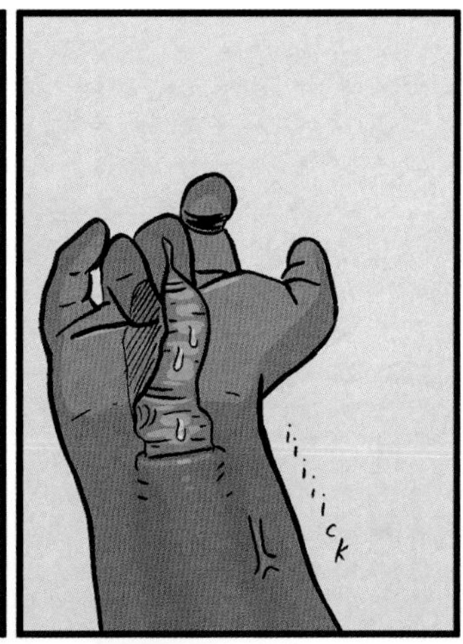
iiiiiiick

WILSON
hyugh

That explains ... all the CARROTS...

WELL, I'M DONE WITH THAT.
WILSON
CLINK

BLEUGHHH

IT'S TOTALLY FINE! IT TASTES JUST LIKE A REGULAR CARROT!!

WEE
OOO
WEE
OOO
WEE
OOO
WEE
WEE OOO
WEE OO
WEE OOO
Get some!
APES
YOINK
KRSHH!
FWSH!
HYAA!
CAWP2
CCPD
POLICE
huff
huff
SAW
NG
RULEZ

I JUST OUTRAN THE COPS!
SLAM

COOL!
SPORT

YOU MUST BE SO PROUD OF YOURSELF.
A GIRL'S GOTTA MAKE A LIVING!
huff huff

WHERE'S FRED?

HE WENT TO GET GROCERIES.
SPORT

HE PULLS HIS WEIGHT AROUND HERE.
S-SORRY...
I APPROVE, MARY.

WHAT DO YOU APPROVE OF?! I DON'T KNOW WHAT YOU'RE—
SHOP & SHOP

YOU LOOK LIKE AN OLD-TIMEY TRAIN ROBBER.
SHOP

AND I SAID DON'T LEAVE THE APARTMENT!
IT'S DANGEROUS !!!
POKE

I have to SHAVE. My face is ITCHY!
SHOP & SHOP
THANKS
WILSON
AND I HAVE BEEN WEARING THE SAME PAIR OF UNDERWEAR FOR--

OKAY, OKAY, WE GET THE PICTURE.

HERE.
Let's
YOU CAN'T WIN ME OVER WITH--
WILSON

LITTLE BAGS OF POTATO CHIPS ...

munch munch

SO... WHO WANTS PAELLA FOR DINNER?
YAY!!
hrmph!
RICE

COULD YOU TURN THAT DOWN?

AHHH!

GLORBONS FROM KROMULE 5 RAVAGE CITY
BREAKING NEWS
LIVE
CNN

NO PARKING
SG
WHAP
WHAP

CREPE CITY'S MIGHTIEST HERO, THE BRAVE AND SEXY MR. GREAT GUY, SEEMS TO BE OUR ONLY HOPE AGAINST THE GLORBONS.

NOT THE LIBRARY... NOOO.

JESUS! WH-WHAT'S GOING ON?

AN ALIEN INVASION IN MIDTOWN CREPE CITY.
JOE SIXPACK IS TAKING A BREAK FROM BATTLING THE **GLORBONS** TO ENJOY A REFRESHING CAN OF **DORIS LITE**, CREPE CITY'S FAVORITE **BEER**.

I'M JUST A REGULAR GUY... UNTIL I DRINK SOME **DORIS LITE**!

GLUG
GLUG

THEN...
CRRR

I CAN FLY!!

GOOD LUCK, JOE!

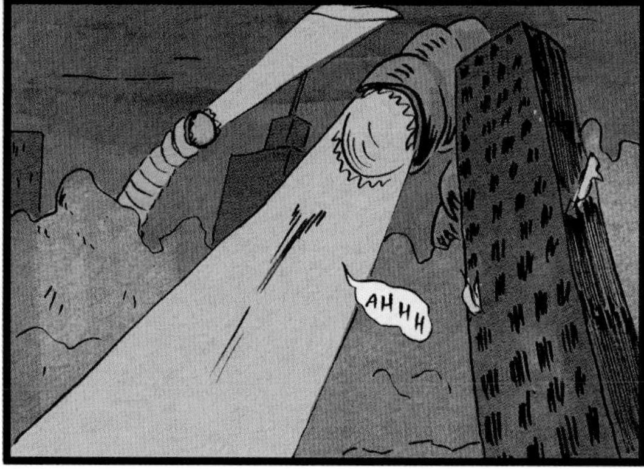
AHHH

FOR ONCE I'M **GLAD** WE LIVE ALL THE WAY OUT HERE. EVERYONE'S ALWAYS SAYING HOW **UNCOOL** THE OUTER BOROUGHS ARE...
RING RING RING
BUT OH **GOD**, ALL THOSE **PEOPLE**...

MOM, DAD, I'M **FINE**! YES. WE'RE ALL SAFE. I WON'T. I **WON'T**!
...WHY WOULD I GO TO WORK TODAY? OF **COURSE** IT'S CANCELED.
ring ring

I LOVE YOU TOO.
PLEASE, DON'T WORRY ABOUT ME, GUYS. I KNOW, IT'S SCARY. I LOVE YOU TOO.

PARENTS, AM I RIGHT?
THEY MEAN WELL. BUT THEY'RE FREAKING ME **OUT**.
BEEP!

MUST BE MY FOLKS.

CREPIZON 7:14
M. BUTTERFLY
I've set up a deal with the aliens in case humanity can't defeat them, don't worry Butterfly Gang. I strongly advise you to stay outside of the affected zones. The casino heist will be postponed until further notice.

IT'S WORK. THEY CANCELED THE **CASINO HEIST.** THIS MUST BE **REALLY** BIG.
LIVE

MAYBE YOU SHOULD CALL YOUR **PARENTS.** THEY'RE PROBABLY WORRIED ABOUT YOU.

WHY SHOULD ***I*** HAVE TO CALL **THEM** WHEN **YOUR** PARENTS CALLED ***YOU***?
I DUNNO, MARY, LIFE'S NOT FAIR.

CREPIZON 7:18
RINGTONES
Doo Wop a Rama
Play Ringt
OTHER RING
Sound of Silence
Horrible Beeps
Club Disco Dance
Rag Time Warp
Flirty Flutes of Babylon

HOLD ON, I'M GETTING A CALL.
doo doo doo

MOM? OH, HUSH YOUR CRYING, I'M FINE.
YES, WE'RE SAFE. LOVE YOU TOO.

...

STOP BEING A CHILD. CALL YOUR PARENTS ALREADY.
I-I JUST **SPOKE** TO THEM!

LEAVE ME ALONE!
MONDAYS

GEEZ.
I SHOULD BE OUT THERE. HELPING MR. GREAT GUY, AND FROOZIE, AND SUPERLADY, AND THE REST OF THE FAIRNESS FEDERATION.

I WISH THERE WERE SOMETHING WE COULD DO. BUT IT'S PROBABLY BEST TO LEAVE THIS TO THE PROS. NO OFFENSE.
LIVE

I JUST WISH MY POWERS WERE BETTER! I FEEL SO... USELESS.
LOOKS LIKE THERE'S LOOTING. HOW LONG IS OUR FOOD GONNA LAST?

I CAN M-MAKE CARROTS...

YOU GUYS ARE FREAKING ME OUT!
I DOTH DETEST MONDAYS

I'M GOING TO THE CORNER STORE TO BUY SOME SNACKS.
I DOTH DETEST M

LIVE
PLAM!

...AND OUR **FIGHTING SPIRIT**, OUR GREAT WILL TO **SURVIVE**, IS WHAT MAKES HUMANITY--
FWWW
NO PARKING

WISK!
LANA !!

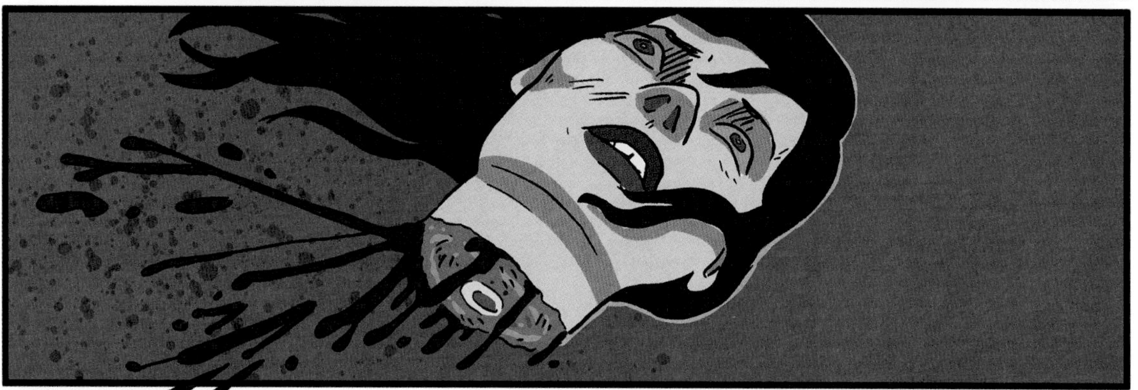

NOOOOO!

OH, GOD--!

YOU'RE GOING TO BE ALL RIGHT...

Y-YOU'RE GOING TO BE ALL RIGHT!
SIZZZZZ

CNN

FWOOOOOOOOOO
KRRR...

IT'S AN INSIDE JOB.
Johnny's MART
LOTTO $1000 winner!

59
$1.50

The Crepe City Times

It's news, okay?

ALIENS DEFEATED!

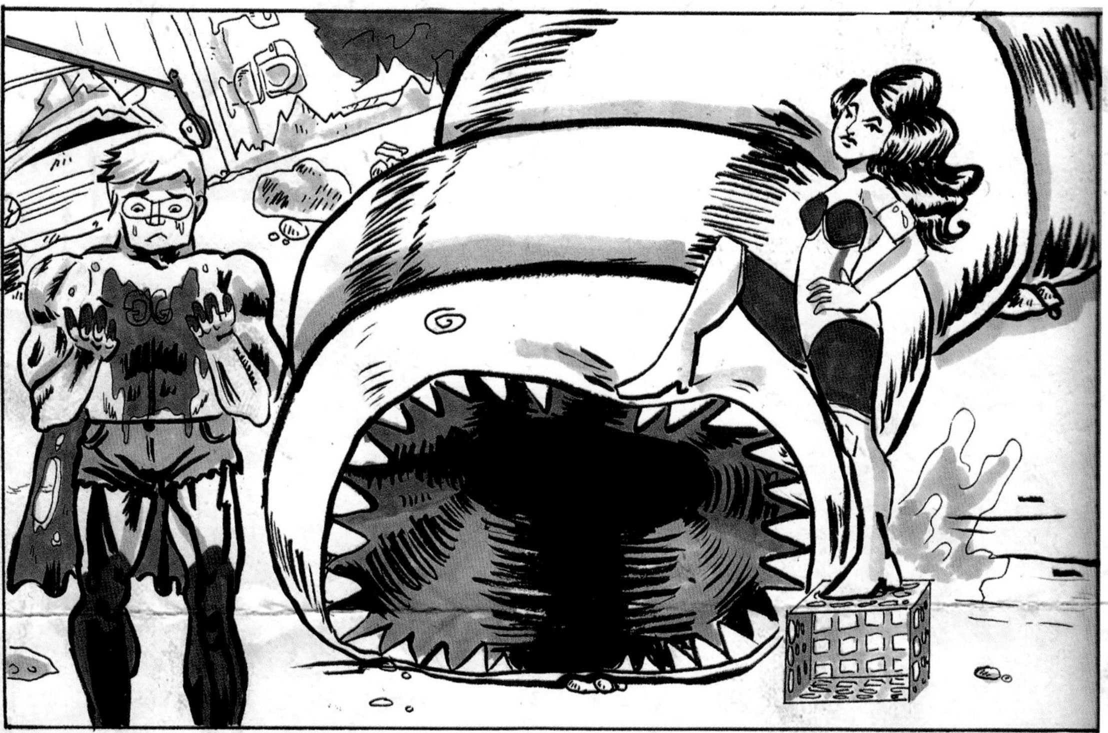

Our heroes bask in the glory of victory. Mr. Great Guy and Superlady celebrate atop the fallen Glorbons. (Photo courtesy of Jonny Jolsen)

Crepe City Mourns

IN MEMORIAM

ST. CREPICIUS ORPHANAGE MOVES TO BETTER FACILITY

Citizen outrage turns to donations, millions raised (B6)

JEWEL OF ALETHEIA MOVED TO CREPE CITY NATURAL HISTORY MUSEUM

"Hope no one steals it," says curator (D15)

Lana Street

Froozie

Thousands of Random Citizens

HENCHGIRL

BY KRISTEN GUDSNUK

THE BUTTERFLY DEN
NO PARKING

SO YOU'RE SAYING THIS CHEMICAL, **L-47...**

WILL SOMEHOW HELP YOU IDENTIFY THE **MOLE** IN THE **CREPICIUS** OPERATION.
YES, AND **GAINTECH'S** HIGH-SECURITY LAB IS THE ONLY PLACE IN CREPE CITY THAT HAS L-47 STOCKED. IT'S **MILITARY-GRADE STUFF.**

NO, I UNDERSTAND **THAT** PART.
WHAT I DON'T UNDERSTAND IS HOW A **CHEMICAL** WILL FIND THE MOLE.

IT'S...
IT'S **SECRET!**

I CAN'T TELL YOU!
YOU MIGHT BE THE MOLE, CHRIS!
GOD!

MONSIEUR BUTTERFLY, TELL HIM!
EVIL PLAN
① Steal L-47
② Find mole
③ ????
Sigh
IT'S SECRET, CHRIS.

I DON'T UNDERSTAND WHAT I BRING TO THIS OPERATION.
ARE THERE SOME HEAVY BOXES THAT NEED LIFTING OR SOMETHING?

YOU'RE CLEARLY HERE FOR YOUR TACTICAL SKILLS.

HUH?

...AND YOUR VAST INTELLECT.
OH, OKAY.

OH MY GOD, SARCASM!
YOU'RE HERE FOR YOUR BRUTISH STRENGTH!
IN CASE OUR NEMESIS MR. GREAT GUY SHOWS UP!

STOP SHIRKING YOUR DUTIES!

MY ROOMMATE WORKS AT GAINTECH.
IT'S A CONFLICT OF INTEREST OR SOMETHING.

WELL, THAT SOLVES THE PROBLEM OF GETTING IN.
TAKE HER ACCESS CARD. THAT WAY WE WON'T SET OFF ANY ALARMS.
I CAN'T DO THAT!

SHE'S MY FRIEND! SHE'LL GET IN TROUBLE!

EITHER YOU DO IT OR WE DO IT. WHICH DO YOU PREFER?
GULP

SIGH . . .

SIIIGHH . . .

LOOK ALIVE, MARY!
IT'S RIGHT HERE.
MICE STACKS
STACKS OF MICE. SCIENCE ABSTRACT
GRAPHS, GRAPHED
MAGGIE
FIRE

SWIPE INTO THIS ROOM, MARY.

Beep

AHA!

L-47

MISSION ACCOMPLISHED!

EUGH, WHAT IS THAT SMELL?
IT SMELLS LIKE... CHEAP WHISKEY AND PEE.

OH GOD. EWWWW.
L-47

STOP ...

RIGHT ...

There.

MY FOE!
MR. GREAT GUY! HOW ARE YOU ALWAYS FOILING MY PLANS?!

Yer evil and muzz be stopped.

STEP ASIDE, MONSIEUR BUTTERFLY.
CHK!

AHH!
PEW!

Oh Lana...
Come back to me

HYUGH

YOU USED TO BE SO . . .
GREAT.
THIS IS JUST PATHETIC. THERE IS NO PLEASURE IN THIS VICTORY.

SEÑOR GREAT GUY!!

AB-
ABUELITA?!
WHAT ARE YOU--
¿SEÑOR GREAT GUY?
Shuffle
Shuffle

ANOTHER ENEMY!
Pew!
?

NOOOOOOOOO
KZATT

WHY ARE YOU SHOOTING AT A LITTLE OLE LADY?!
SIZZ

SHE'S THE ENEMY.

GET AWAY FROM HER!
¿ESTÁS BIEN?

YAH!
BOOF!

JESUS.

I AM LA MUCAMA!
CREPE CITY'S NEWEST HERO!

TRUSTY SIDEKICK TO MR. GREAT GUY...

OW.
HOW'S THIS FOR A SIDE KICK?!
POW!

Okay...

WE HAVE WHAT WE CAME HERE FOR.

hahaha!
PEW! PEW!
Lana...
LET'S GET OUT BEFORE THE COPS...
WHATEVER.

YOU STOLE MY ACCESS CARD!
YOU PUT MY JOB, MY REPUTATION IN JEOPARDY!
YOU'RE SO--

SELFISH!! UGH!

OH... OH, DON'T MAKE THAT FACE.

LOOK, YOU JUST... YOU'VE GOTTA STOP COMMITTING CRIMES.
OR AT LEAST DON'T GET ME INVOLVED.
ARE YOU M-MAD AT ME?

YES.
YES, I'M MAD AT YOU.

WAHH

WAIT, NO, I'M NOT MAD AT YOU.
hic

98

THE CHEMISTRY OF LOVE

FLAME GIRL AND **EL ROMANCERO** WROTE A **BOOK.**

UH, WHAT?
THE SUPERHEROES FROM THE '80S. THEY SAVED NEW FORK CITY FROM BLOWING UP THAT ONE TIME.
THEY'RE GONNA BE AT THE BOOKSTORE THIS AFTERNOON.

SIGNING **THIS.**
A Super Family
A MEMOIR
FLAME GIRL
EL ROMANCERO

I KNOW WHO THEY ARE. ARE YOU SURE YOU SHOULD GO TO SOMETHING AS **WELL ATTENDED** AS A **BOOK SIGNING?**
AREN'T YOU ON THE LAM?
MY DISGUISE IS FLAWLESS!

YOU KNOW WHO YOU SHOULD TAKE WITH YOU?
MARY.

YEAH, OKAY, WHATEVER.
shrug

Believe
Achieve
You can!
NO NO NO NO NO
NO NO

IT'S NOT SAFE.
YOU SHOULDN'T.
YOU CAN'T.
NOOOOOOO
MARY...

no no no no no
THAT IS
GETTING REALLY
ANNOYING.
Fall into
Reading

THANK YOU ALL
FOR COMING TODAY!

ROMAN AND I WOULD LIKE TO PRESENT A SPECIAL GUEST!
OUR WONDERFUL DAUGHTER, **PHOTO-GIRL!**
SIGNI
TODAY
4-6

SAY CHEESE!

wooo!
I love you
clap clap

"OUTGUNNED, OUTNUMBERED."

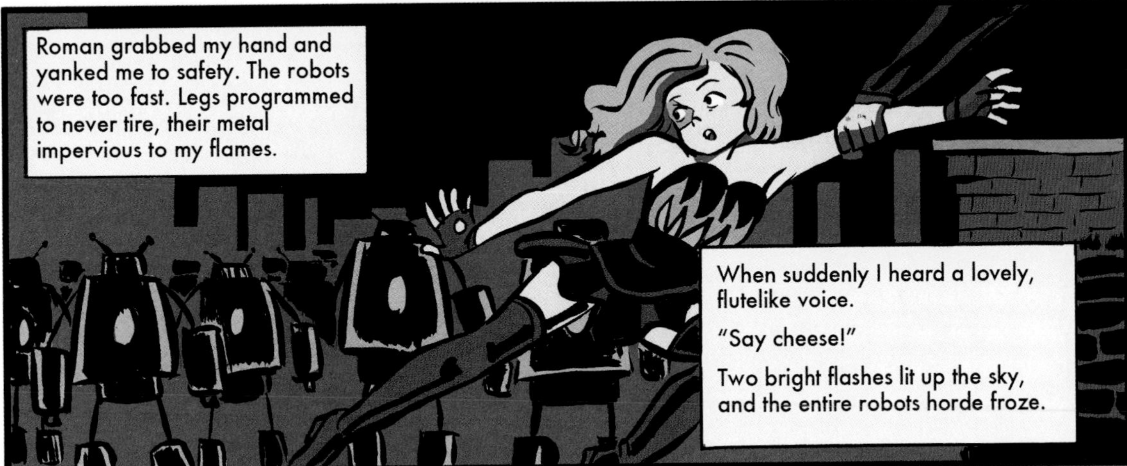
Roman grabbed my hand and yanked me to safety. The robots were too fast. Legs programmed to never tire, their metal impervious to my flames.
When suddenly I heard a lovely, flutelike voice.
"Say cheese!"
Two bright flashes lit up the sky, and the entire robots horde froze.

"Why aren't you in school, young lady?" Roman teased her.
SPELLS
"I figured... you could use my help..." Photo-Girl replied, straining to hold the hundreds of robots captive.

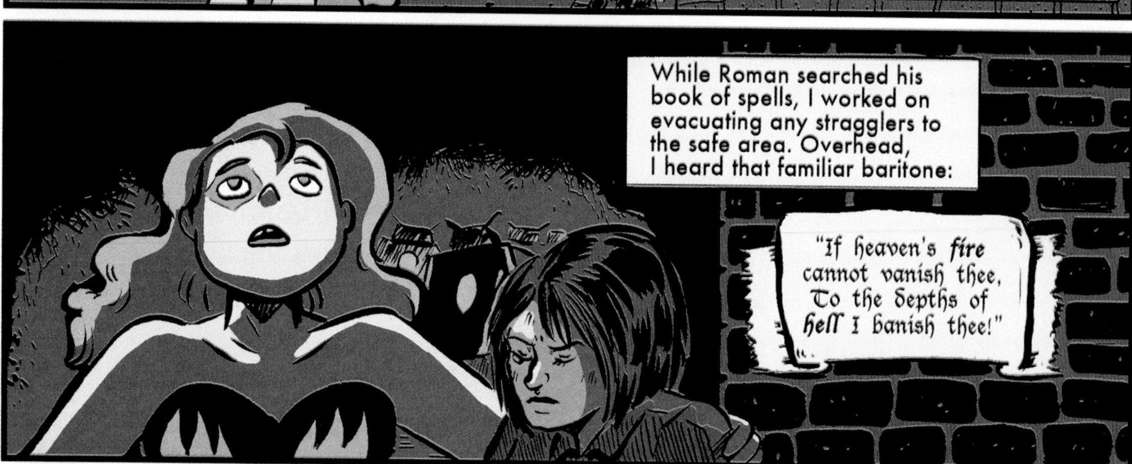
While Roman searched his book of spells, I worked on evacuating any stragglers to the safe area. Overhead, I heard that familiar baritone:
"If heaven's fire cannot vanish thee, To the depths of hell I banish thee!"

WHY IS SHE DOING ALL THE READING?
I CAME HERE TO HEAR EL ROMANCERO!
Seriously!

IF HE HAD READ THAT SPELL ALOUD, WE'D ALL BE BANISHED TO THE DEPTHS OF HELL.
and you call yourselves FANS!

"SOME PARENTS GET THEIR DAUGHTER A CAR FOR HER SIXTEENTH BIRTHDAY.
"A FEW MONTHS BEFORE, FLAME GIRL AND I HAD LUCKILY DECIDED THAT HOVERJET MIGHT PROVE MORE USEFUL TO OUR VERY SPECIAL DAUGHTER.

"AND HOW THANKFUL WE HAVE BEEN FOR THAT DECISION EVER SINCE--THE COUNTLESS TIMES OUR SUPER DAUGHTER HAS COME TO OUR AID.

"FAMILY IS THE ONE THING WE HOLD ABOVE ALL ELSE.

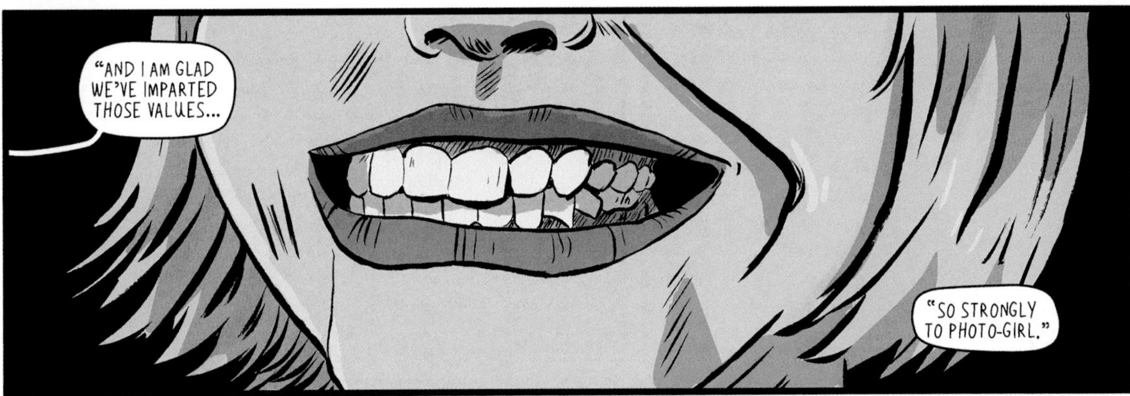
"AND I AM GLAD WE'VE IMPARTED THOSE VALUES...
"SO STRONGLY TO PHOTO-GIRL."

THE FIFTH CHILD

WOW, IT'S SO NICE TO FINALLY MEET YOU! I'VE HEARD SUCH GREAT THINGS!
UH... THANK YOU!
WHO SHOULD I SIGN THIS TO?
MUST READ

SIGN IT...

You mean "whom"!
TO MARY!

To Mary
Thank

I SAID **MARY!!!**

?!!
Hi... parents.

YOU **ALWAYS** HAVE TO MAKE A **SPECTACLE,** DON'T YOU.

Um...

OK BYE

YOU'RE **STAYING!** C'MON!
Y-YEAH. MAYBE THEY'LL GIVE ME MONEY.

YOUR PARENTS ARE **SUPERHEROES.**

Yeah.

IMAGINE HOW **EASY** IT WOULD BE TO BREAK INTO **HEROISM** WITH FLAME GIRL AND EL ROMANCERO AS YOUR PARENTS.

MY PARENTS WERE **ACCOUNTANTS.**
THAT IS A RESPECTABLE FIELD OF EMPLOYMENT.

BUT...

...you're a villain.
!!

IX-NAY on the ILLAIN-VAY!!
mhm

TINA!!
!!

IX-NAY on the ILLAIN-VAY!!
SHAKE

KILL ME
um

WHAT'S VANILLIN?

wah wah

WHAT'S VANILLIN?

HUH? IT'S A PHENOL DERIVATIVE FOUND IN VANILLA BEANS.

...

FIX YOUR BRA STRAP.

SO, PAIGE MIGHT BECOME NIKOM'S SPOKESPERSON--
MOM!!

NOTHING IS SET IN STONE YET. IT'S ALL DEPENDENT ON MY FAIRNESS FEDERATION APPLICATION.
BESIDES, IT'S NO BIG DEAL.

ha ha ha!
OH, IT'S A BIG DEAL.
A BIG, EXPENSIVE DEAL.
nudge

YOU KEEP THIS UP, YOU'LL BE AS RICH AS GREG GAINS!

I'D JUST BE HAWKING CAMERAS. YOU GOTTA ADMIT IT'S **APPROPRIATE.**
THAT'S... INSANE.

SO NICE TO MEET MARY'S... FRIENDS.
I TRUST SHE PAYS HER RENT ON TIME?

YES, SHE DOES.

OH, I'M SORRY, **EL ROMANCERO**, BUT I'VE BEEN A FAN FOREVER. COULD I GET A PICTURE?
¡POR SUPUESTO!

FLASH!!

Moses Supposes his toeses are Roses ...

FOR YOU.
!!

WHAT A NEAT TRICK. ISN'T THAT **HOW DAD PROPOSED** TO YOU, MOM?

AHEM
WOW, I CAN'T BELIEVE I'M EATING WITH **FLAME GIRL!** I HAD A **POSTER** OF YOU IN MY **BEDROOM** GROWING UP!

...

IT WAS, LIKE, NO BIG DEAL OR ANYTHING. I HAD...
A LOT OF POSTERS. I HAD A POSTER OF A SHARK--

SO IT'S *SUE*, *TINA*, AND...
SORRY, WHAT'S YOUR NAME AGAIN?
no
I'M SUE.
me?
I'm Fred.

AND YOU'RE MARY'S...
"ROOMMATE"?

WELL, IT'S **COMPLICATED.**

fwoooooo o O

NOT LIKE THAT.
YOU SEE...

I'M AN UP-AND-COMING **SUPERHERO**, AND I KINDA GOT ON ONE OF CREPE CITY'S CRIME LORDS' **HIT LIST.**
SO I'VE BEEN HIDING OUT--

WHY DON'T YOU JUST TAKE OUT THE CRIME LORD?

WHY DON'T **YOU** TAKE OUT ALL THE CRIME LORDS?!

W-WOW, THIS BREAD IS REALLY AMAZING!

SO HOW'VE YOU BEEN, PAIGE? I HAVEN'T HEARD FROM YOU IN AGES!

I EMAILED YOU!
DID NOT!

GLITTERGIRL42@YAGOO.COM, NO?

OH MY GOD! I HAVEN'T USED THAT EMAIL ADDRESS SINCE TENTH GRADE!
S-sorry

NOW IT'S GLITTER**WOMAN**42@YAGOO.COM.

Sigh

WELL, LIFE IS KINDA HECTIC. I'M REALLY STRESSED OUT BECAUSE I APPLIED TO THE **FAIRNESS FEDERATION** AND--
YOU WILL GET IN! TRUST ME!

I DO HAVE AN ADVANTAGE, BEING A **LEGACY HERO** AND ALL, BUT IF I DON'T GET IN IT'LL BE ALL THE MORE **HUMILIATING.**
THE *FF* WOULD BE **RIDICULOUS** TO NOT ACCEPT YOU. A GIRL WITH SUCH SPECTACULAR POWERS AS YOURS--
THE ABILITY TO FREEZE TIME!

...AND AFTER LOSING **FROOZIE** IN THE **GLORBON INVASION,** THEY REALLY NEED NEW MEMBERS.

MY ASSESSMENT DIDN'T GO SO WELL. YOU SHOULD HAVE SEEN THE COMPETITION. THERE WAS A GUY WHO COULD ABSORB MOMENTUM.

DON'T WORRY, SWEETIE! I TALKED TO **BRAIN MAN,** AND--
WELL, I GUESS I SHOULD WAIT UNTIL YOU GET THE **OFFICIAL ACCEPTANCE**--

WELCOME TO THE FAIRNESS FEDERATION!

OH MY GOD!!

I'M SO HAPPY!!

clap
CONGRATS
clap
We're so PROUD of you

SO...

WHEN DID YOU TWO FIND TIME TO WRITE THIS BOOK?

IT HAS BEEN ROMAN AND MY PET PROJECT FOR A FEW YEARS NOW.

AM...
AM I IN THE BOOK AT ALL?
smoosh
smoosh

OH, **HONEY**, WE WANTED TO, BUT THE EDITOR SAID IT WOULDN'T FIT THE **NARRATIVE**.
YOU KNOW, **"SUPER-POWERED FAMILY."**

NOT EVEN IN THE **ACKNOWLEDGMENTS?!**

HOW DOES HAVING A **DAUGHTER** IN THE **BUTTERFLY GANG** NOT FIT THE **NARRATIVE**?
YOU'D THINK THAT'D MAKE FOR SOME EXCITING STORYTELLING! A LOT MORE **COMPELLING** THAN--
SLAM!!

TINA MEANS... MARY'S IN... A PLAY...
ABOUT THE BUTTERFLY GANG.
heh

24
CCFD

HEY, GUY! YOU'RE NOT SUPPOSED TO... AW, **HELL.**

I'M SO SORRY I MADE YOU COME. I DON'T KNOW, I IMAGINED, LIKE, A TEARFUL REUNION.
THE GOOD KIND OF TEARFUL REUNION.

I DIDN'T KNOW IT WAS A SECRET.
keff

IT'S NOT YOUR FAULT.

sigh...
AMBU LA
EMERGENCY

SUCH A REBEL.

sniff
OH, STOP RUBBING IT IN.

THEY'LL GET OVER IT.
PROBABLY FASTER IF YOU GET A MORE REPUTABLE JOB THAN BEING A **HENCHGIRL**.

IF ONLY **I** COULD HAVE A **MILLION-DOLLAR CONTRACT**.

...

LET'S NOT WAIT ANOTHER **TWO YEARS** TO SEE EACH OTHER AGAIN, **OKAY?**
HAS IT REALLY BEEN TWO YEARS?
TIME *FLIES* WHEN YOU'RE HAVING FUN.

BUT I WASN'T EVEN HAVING *FUN*.

GUESS IT KEEPS GOING, REGARDLESS.
EMT

HENCHGIRL

KICK
ME

Chicanery Hooliganism Subterfuge

mountain range

By
KRISTEN
GUDSNUK

HENCHGIRL

KRISTEN GUDSNUK

CAFE
FREE
KAZ 2Y5
sigh

PALAWAN!

GEEZ! DID YOU GET CAUGHT IN THE INVASION OR SOMETHING?
DOES IT LOOK BAD?!

HEY, IT'LL PROBABLY TURN INTO SOME TOUGH-LOOKING SCARS!

THEY THOUGHT I WAS THE MOLE. FOR THE ORPHANAGE.
I GUESS I HAD THE MOST MOTIVE, GROWING UP THERE AND ALL.

SO... THE BUTTERFLY GANG DID THIS TO YOU?

I THOUGHT I WAS GONNA DIE.
PUSH

PIZZA
HI, WE'RE HERE FOR THE **PROTECTION PAYMENT** COLLECTION.

I'LL GO GET DA BOSS.

SWISH

VOOMP
PLEASE DON'T A-**HURT** ME! I DON'T HAVE ALL THE **MONEY** YET!

HEY, IT'S JUST **US.** DON'T WORRY.

OH, GRAZIE A DIO!
I THOUGHT IT A-WAS YOUR **COMPAGNOS,** THE MEAN ONES!

THEY'RE COMING NEXT WEEK.

THEY A-**BROKE** MY NEPHEW'S **THUMB**! HOW HE A-MAKE **PIZZA** ANYMORE?

I'M STUCK AT DA **REGISTER** NOW. IT'S NOT AS FULFILLING.

LOOK, JUST GIVE US WHAT YOU CAN. IT'S NO BIG DEAL.

IT IS NOT VERY MUCH ...
A-THANK YOU!

HERE, YOU GET FREE CREPE PIZZA!
WE COULDN'T!

I INSIST!
Well ...
If you INSIST ...

SO HOW DID YOU CONVINCE THEM YOU WEREN'T THE MOLE?
JUST REPEATED "I DIDN'T DO IT" A LOT. MUSTA SUNK IN AFTER A FEW HOURS.
SGUZZLE

GEEZ. I'M SO SORRY, PAL.
DON'T BE. I'M GLAD THE PLAN FAILED. IT WAS STUPID.
I WOULDA LEAKED IT IF I KNEW HOW TO GO ABOUT LEAKING THINGS.

HEY, HEY, I AGREE WITH YOU. IT WAS A NEEDLESSLY CRUEL PLAN.
I MEAN, I DIDN'T SIGN UP TO BE PART OF THE CHAINSAW GANG. I JUST WANT TO ROB BUSINESSES AND RICH PEOPLE. NOT... ORPHANS.
MHM!
CHOKING RULES
• NO CHOKING

SPECIAL
ha
I MEAN, DOES COCO HAVE A SCREW LOOSE OR SOMETHING?
WHY WOULD SHE THINK THAT WAS A GOOD IDEA?!

I THINK IT MIGHT HAVE BEEN BEFORE YOUR TIME, BUT IF YOU CAN BELIEVE IT, COCO USED TO BE TOTALLY **NORMAL.**
YOU'RE **LYING!**

NOT THE **FRIENDLIEST** GIRL ON THE PLANET, BUT NONE OF THIS PSYCHOPATH CRAP.
IT'S LIKE SOMEONE REPLACED HER **BRAIN!**

"Abby Normal."

skrish

MENU
BEST of 2002
YOU WERE THE MOLE.

nooooo.

Okay.

uh

OKAY, LIKE, FOR INSTANCE, I'M FINE ROBBING **THAT** GUY.
ZZA
CLUNK

PIZZA
ME TOO.
beep!

PIZZA
OPEN
hmm...
YOU'RE GOING TO BE ALL RIGHT.

...AND I DON'T GET WHY PEOPLE TAKE THE WHOLE WALLET.
CANCELING CREDIT CARDS IS SUCH A **HASSLE!**

IZZA
NOT TO MENTION GETTING A NEW **LICENSE** OR **ID**! YOU HAVE TO GO TO...

THE DMV!!
They have such inconvenient hours!

wow! Thanks!

BUTTERFLY GANG!!

hi!!
yay!

DO BUTTERFLY ZAP!

WANT ME TO ZAP THAT TREE?
Yeah!

BUTTERFLY ZAP!
BZZT!
CAN WE SEE YOUR GUN, MISTER?
NOW, KIDS, GUNS AREN'T TOYS.

YOU SEE, THERE'S A MINIATURE ELECTRIC SHOCK DEVICE ATTACHED TO MY WRIST!
IT'S SILK!
THAT'S NOT A REAL GUN!

STRING SHOT!
SQUILCH!

BEEP!
BEEP!

4:00 PM
M. BUTTERFLY
COME TO BUTTERFLY DEN ASAP!!!! >:(

yay!

SAY
CHEESE

HOP ON!
...

Pat
pat

CAN'T I DRIVE?!
NOPE!

SHOP ♡
4-EVA!

THE BUTTERFLY DEN
CHAINSAW
GANG
RULEZ
CRRK!

CLIK
SORRY WE'RE LATE, WE GOT STUCK IN--

I DID IT!
I FOUND MANNEQUIN!

HE TURNED INTO A STATUE OR SOMETHIN'.
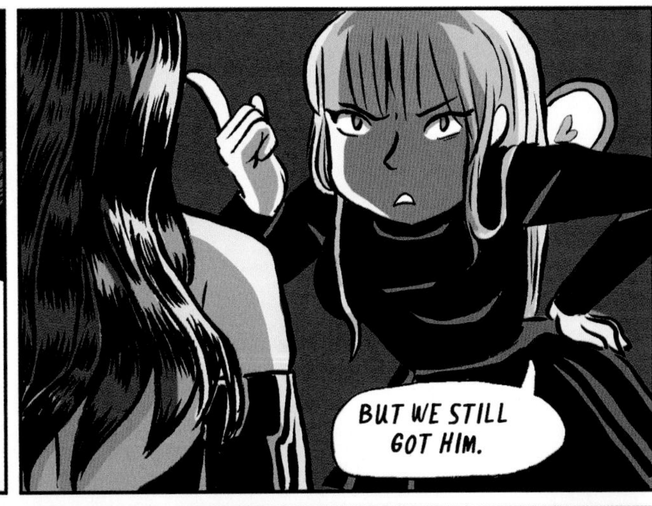
BUT WE STILL GOT HIM.

OH. GOOD.

AND RIGHT BEFORE HE SHATTERED . . .

HE TOLD US WHO THE MOLE WAS.

HUH? HE DID? WHO WAS THE MOLE?

...

Knavery is up 15% but hooliganism has plummeted 20%.

GUESS THAT'S IT! GREAT WORK, TEAM.
DRINKS ARE ON ME. LET'S GO TO THE BAR!

CONSERVATION
'05
Y-YOU GUYS ARE JUST GONNA LEAVE EVIDENCE ON THE GROUND?!

I CAN VACUUM HIM UP TOMORROW.

SUPPLY
B-BUT--!
NO, I'VE GOT IT.

WOULD YOU TWO STOP SQUABBLING OVER EVERY LITTLE THING?

IT'S TIME FOR A CELEBRATION!
...AND HOW OFTEN DO WE HAVE REASON TO CELEBRATE AROUND HERE?

FINE! HAVE FUN DISPOSING THE BODY!
YEP.

ARE YOU OKAY?
LEAVE ME ALONE.

Okay...
EVIL SCHEME

THAT'S CONVENIENT!
SWISH
GRAVE PLOTS SOLD HERE

How can ya fix this broken guy
KRRR
SALE
MUST ARD

how come a loser never wins?
FIRST AI
HAIR TIES
krrr

Please help me fix my shattered life
SCHOOL SUPPLIES

and help me live once more.
KRAGLE
BESTGLUE
TAPE
GLUE

Pthump
OPEN

GLUE
GLUE
KRAZY GLUE

TAKE IT YOU BROKE SOMETHING?
CIG

THIS COULD WORK.
LOGICALLY.
VROOOOOOO
YEAH.

SIGH

MARY! YOU'RE HOME!
TELL ME ALL ABOUT YOUR EXCITING ADVENTURES!

Uh...

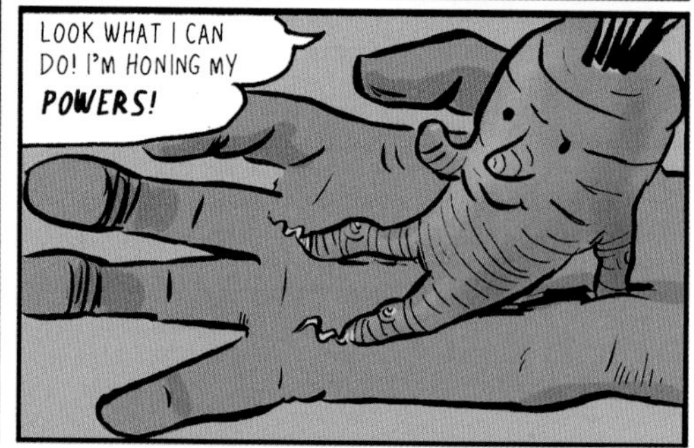
LOOK WHAT I CAN DO! I'M HONING MY POWERS!

Er... that's... ummm very nice...

OK good night

SHE DIDN'T MEAN IT! PLEASE DON'T CRY!

FRED . . .
THAT'S LIFE
I ASSUME YOU'RE HOVERING OVER ME, LIKE SOME ASTRAL-PLANE GUARDIAN ANGEL, SO IF YOU ARE, I'M TALKING TO YOU.
IF YOU'RE NOT, WELL, THAT DOESN'T MAKE SENSE. YOU DIDN'T *DIE*, BECAUSE YOU LEFT YOUR BODY, CLEARLY. BASED ON THIS PILE OF BROKEN PLASTER.
SO YOU'RE OUT THERE. AND YOU'RE PROBABLY HERE, BECAUSE YOU MUST BE CURIOUS ABOUT THE FATE OF YOUR CORPOREAL SELF.
ANYWAY. I AM GOING TO PUT YOU BACK TOGETHER. THAT SHOULD WORK. REMEMBER YOU SAID YOUR ARM COULD COME OFF IF SOMEONE TOUCHED YOU-- SOMETHING LIKE THAT--
I MEAN, HOW WOULD YOU KNOW THAT IF NOT FROM EXPERIENCE?
RIGHT? IF YOU'VE BEEN ***BROKEN*** BEFORE, IT STANDS TO REASON THAT YOU'VE BEEN FIXED ***BEFORE***!

SQUICK!
CRKK!
WHAT ARE YOU MADE OF, **PORCELAIN?**
SERIOUSLY, FRED, IF THIS WORKS, YOU NEED A **POWER UPGRADE.**
BEEP
BEEP
AUGHH!
IT'S ALL WRONG
I DON'T KNOW WHAT THIS IS SUPPOSED TO **BE**!! THEY ALL LOOK THE **SAME**!!!
BEEP
SIGH
Search THE WEB
HUMAN ANATOMY
CREPIPEDIA - HUMAN A
SCIENCE 4 KIDZ
XXX GIRLS - live human anatomy
CLICKKK

BEEP!!
Kneecap

yawn!
BEEP

WELL, FRED, **YOU'RE** LOOKING A WHOLE LOT BETTER.
A WHOLE LOT MORE WHOLE.

sexy guy
CAN I BORROW YOUR--

Blow dryer?
sexy guy

GET OUT!

KEEP THE STUPID BLOW DRYER !!!

NOW, WHERE WERE WE.
KNEECAP.
oh...
HOW DID I NOT SEE IT BEFORE ?!
BEEP
UGH!

CREPIZON 8:32 PM
NEW MESSAGES:
Mon B: WHERE R U SRSLY??! >:(
Mon B: So late its not funny
Mon B: Get here NOW
Mon B: is everything OK??
Mon B: Mary? Did u forget?
Mon B: The heist at Crepe City Bank. 42 Caroline Street... u lost again?
Mon B: You're late Mary :/
Mon B: Heist time! Grab your empty money bags
Mon B: You guys excited for heist tonight? :) I AM!
MORE NEW MESSAGES

Sigh...

NOW, YOU'RE GONNA TELL US THE COMBINATION TO THE VAULT, OR OLD MRS. PEVENSIE GETS A TASTE OF MY BLADE.
GOODNESS!
ABRE UNA CUENTA DE AHORRO HOY!
TAP TAP

THIS ISN'T WORKING, COCO.
I TAKE IT YOU HAVE A BETTER--

YAGH!
VAULT
GROAN

CREAK!

!
grumble grumble
MONEY

YOU'RE WELCOME.
CREPE CITY BANK: a family business

VAULT
fwish
goodness!
STOMPSTOM

GRR!

HOLY COW.
IT'S **DONE.**

FRED, YOU CAN
COME BACK NOW.

AUGH!!
YOU MISSED A SPOT--
SPLURT
FRED!

FIX... THE HOLE...
IN MY CHEST...

THAT'S LIFE!
OKAY!
FIRST LET'S...
COVER YOU
UP...

NOW, MAYBE IF I JUST FILL THE HOLE WITH SOME GLUE?

FWOOO
WAS I ...DEAD?

I HAVE NO IDEA.

OH MAN, I'M SO GLAD YOU'RE OKAY!
OW

COMFY?
YEAH...

YOU'RE GOING TO BE FINE.
TH-THANKS.

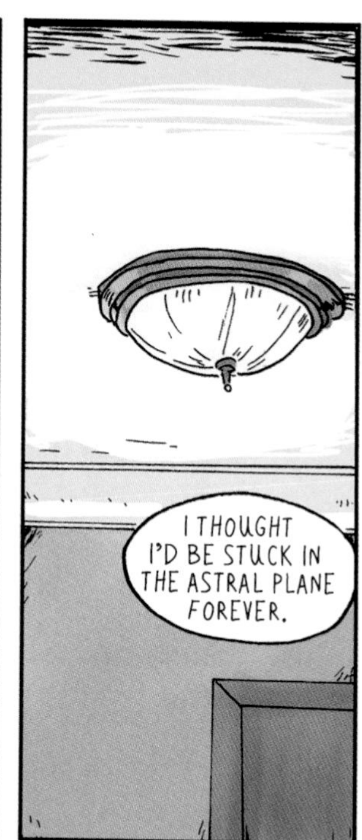
I THOUGHT I'D BE STUCK IN THE ASTRAL PLANE FOREVER.

THANKS FOR PUTTING ME BACK TOGETHER.

I'M THE ONE WHO GOT YOU **BROKEN** IN THE FIRST PLACE.
NAH, IT WAS ALL THOSE **ORPHANS'** FAULT.

?!

KIDDING!
OH!
T'S LIFE
RTH IT!

I DON'T **BLAME** YOU, MARY.

I THINK YOU'RE THE ONLY PERSON WHO'D BOTHER TO GLUE ME BACK TOGETHER.

DEFINITELY THE ONLY **GIRL** WHO'D BOTHER.

SUPER GLUE **IS** SURPRISINGLY EXPENSIVE.

LIFE!

WORTH IT
LIFE!

STILL ALIVE!

HENCHGIRL
BY KRISTEN GUDSNUK
GUIDE
INFO

SCIENCE
Jewel of Aletheia
CREPE CITY MUSEUM of NATURAL HISTORY
WE'RE IN! OVER!

AGHH! YOU WALK TOO SLOW!

IT'S CALLED **STEALTH.** TRY IT SOMETIME.

CRABS!
THE GRID IS DOWN. OVER.

ROGER THAT, MONSIEUR B.

WOO!

CLAP CLAP

QUIET! THIS IS A STEALTH MISSION!!

CRAP!

I GOT THIS.
GEEZ!

Hey!
THAT'S A BIT MUCH, DON'T YOU THINK?!

meh.

AND WHERE WERE YOU EVEN HIDING THAT THING?!

TIP TIP TIP
SLEEPY TIME.
THUMP!

YOU REALLY NEED A NEW CATCH PHRASE.

I THINK THIS JEWEL OF ALETHEIA THING IS IN THE GREEK WING, RIGHT? OR IS IT IN THE MINERALS SECTION?

HMPH...
OH, MARY. PREPARED AS USUAL. IT'S UP TWO FLIGHTS, IN GEOLOGY.
MUSEUM GUIDE

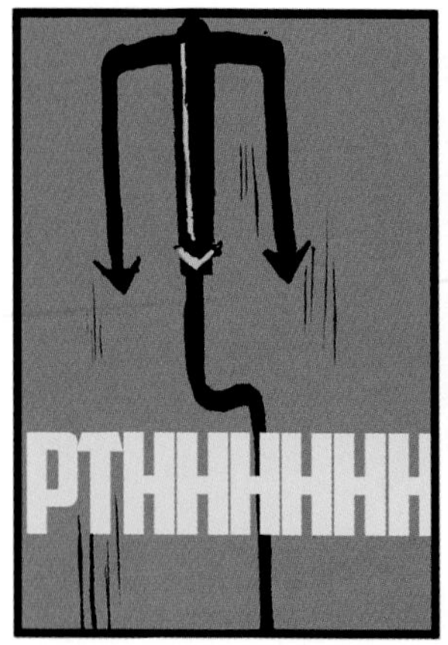
PTHHHHHH

FFFFF
TO THE GEOLOGY FLOOR!

Show off.

CAFE
huff huff
SERIOUSLY.

I CUT OFF POWER TO THE MUSEUM'S ALARMS, BUT THE JEWEL SEEMS TO HAVE **EXTRA PROTECTION.**
THE JEWEL OF ALETHEIA

WE COULD PROBABLY GRAB IT AS LONG AS WE DON'T TRIP THE—
ASTEROIDS ARE COOL

OKAY!

NOT **YOU,** SAUSAGE FINGERS!
SAUSAGE FINGERS?

GOT IT.
LET'S SPLIT.
FLPPP

GREAT. SORRY WE ROUGHED YOU UP, BUD. WE REALLY THOUGHT YOU LEAKED THE ORPHANAGE SCAM. YOU REALLY DIDN'T DO IT, HUH?
I SWEAR IT WASN'T ME!

...

HEY, MARY, YOU'VE DONE ABSOLUTELY NOTHING OF MERIT ON THIS MISSION.
WHY DON'T YOU AT LEAST CARRY THE JEWEL OF ALETHEIA BACK TO THE BUTTERFLY DEN?
I SAVED THAT ONE GUY BEFORE ...

I... I REALLY DIDN'T ...
FINE.

ALL THIS EFFORT FOR SOME DUMB ROCK.
IT'S NOT EVEN THAT SHINY.

hmph!

MARY, DID YOU LEAK THE ORPHANAGE OPERATION?

WE'VE GOT OUR **CULPRIT.**

VRHHH
I DIDN'T **DO** IT!

squirm
squirm
REALLY I DIDN'T!
I THOUGHT--
I THOUGHT YOU SAID, "DID **HUGH** LEAK THE ORPHANAGE SCHEME?"
LIKE, YOU KNOW, THAT GUY HUGH...
...
DO YOU KNOW HUGH?

THE **JEWEL OF ALETHEIA** IS A STONE WITH **MAGICAL** PROPERTIES, **MARY**. IT CAUSES ITS BEARER TO TELL THE TRUTH. IF YOU HAD **BOTHERED** TO LOOK UP WHAT WE WERE STEALING... WELL, THEN YOU MIGHT HAVE REALIZED IT WAS A **TRAP**.
nngh...
LORD CTHULU

KLONK
KLONK
KLONK
I THINK SOMEONE SWITCHED IT OUT WITH A ROCK THAT MAKES YOU LIE!

GAHHH!
IF YOU DAMAGE THE BUTTERFLY BUGGIE, SO HELP ME--

HELP!

BZZT!
BUTT
KRRR

FZZZ
heh.

WHY DON'T WE JUST WASTE HER NOW? THE RIVER'S RIGHT OVER THERE.
WE WOULDN'T EVEN HAVE TO BURY HER.
WHY MAKE IT A WHOLE THING?

SHE'S A TRAITOR, AND SHE'S TOTALLY LAZY AND WORTHLESS.
SHE'S WORSE THAN LARRY, AND LARRY IS JUST THE WORST.
DONUTS 24HR
LOANS
THAT'S NOT MY STYLE. I HAVE A BETTER WAY OF DEALING WITH OVERLY PRINCIPLED HENCHGIRLS. TIME TO PAY A VISIT TO . . . DR. MANIAC!

GONNA EUTHANIZE ME, THEN? THAT'S REMARKABLY HUMANE.

AGH! WHAT IS THIS ROPE MADE OUT OF, MITHRIL?!
CAN'T YOU TASE HER AGAIN?

SAVOR THESE MOMENTS. WHO KNOWS, YOU MIGHT MISS HER.
HA HA HA!
Yeah... maybe not.

Florist for the Trees
EUGENE MANIAC, MD
"Nothing to See Here!"
BUTT

ASK US ABOUT Assisted Suicide
FREE PAMPHLE
for Your Health
Littering is FUN!
SUPPORT THE PATRIARCHY
Demon Blood-Getting Started
Abortion Séances

← OFFICE 1A - 1G
HELLO... DOCTOR.

HERE'S THE **L-47** YOU REQUESTED.

EXCELLENT.

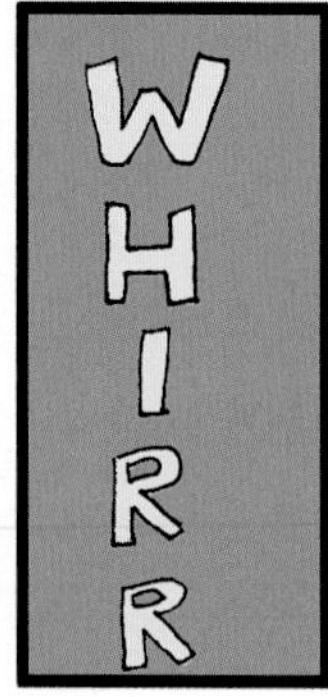
WHIRR

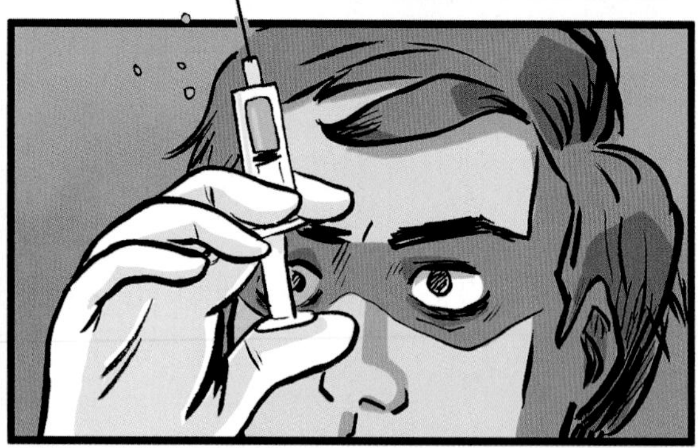

DON'T WORRY. I'VE TESTED THIS FORMULA *EXTENSIVELY.*

Even on **MYSELF.**

WAIT, ***HUH?*** IT'S NOT ***LETHAL?*** SO YOU'RE NOT... GOING TO ***KILL*** ME?

How do you Keep doing that?!!
noo...
YOU DIDN'T TELL HER WHAT WE'RE ***DOING?***

LOOK AT THIS FRIGHTENED LITTLE LAMB.
BAA
NOW, JUST LOOK AT THAT POSTER OVER THERE.
YOU'LL JUST FEEL A LITTLE **STING.**
Hang in There

WHAF?!

whaf did you... do...

to...

AND EVERYONE **LAUGHED** WHEN I INVENTED **MEMORY-ERASING KNOCKOUT LOLLIPOPS!**

OR AT LEAST... I **THINK** I INVENTED THEM.

Crepe City.
Flattened into a sad French pancake.

A sad, sad, sad pancake.

GAINS MANOR, THE OUTSKIRTS OF CREPE CITY
The skyline still in ruins from— FROM—!!

Oh... Lana.

TO THINK I WAS ONCE ASHAMED OF MY **SCRAPBOOKING** HOBBY...
"the one"
THE VERY THING THAT PRESERVES MY BEAUTIFUL ...
Love Forever
By Lana Street
BEAUTIFUL ...
MEMORIES.

SEÑOR GAINS, YOU HAVE A CALL FROM **SUPERLADY**.
SHE SAYS IT IS VERY **URGENTE**.

sniff

IF YOU NO CONTINUE TO FIGHT CRIME, OTHER **INOCENTÉS** WILL BE HURT.
It's... all... pointless.

SOB
plip plip

POR FAVOR, ABUELITA, DÉJAME MOSTRAR QUE SOY HEROÍNA! PUEDO SER COMO **SUPERLADY**!
TENGO QUE SALVAR A LA GENTE!
NO HAY OTRO REMEDIO.

GO HELP **SUPERLADY**, NIETA. PERO **CUÍDATE**.

HELLO, SUPERLADY?
I CAN FILL IN FOR **MR. GREAT GUY**; HE IS NO FEELING WELL. MY NAME IS...

LA MUCAMA.

Hello.
YAGH!

MARY? IS THAT **YOU?**

This...

IS FOR BREAKING MY **GOGGLES!**

WHAT IS **WRONG** WITH YOU?!
I.
Really.

LIKED.

THOSE.
...

GOGGLES!

THEY STOPPED MANUFACTURING THEM!
NOW I HAVE NO DISGUISE!
THWAK!
AND I DON'T WANT TO FIND A DIFFERENT PAIR OF GOGGLES.

I HOPE YOU'VE LEARNED YOUR LESSON.

HENCHGIRL

BY KRISTEN GUDSNUK

CREPE
CITY
CATERI
FRED! HAVE A SEAT. YOU HADN'T RETURNED MY CALLS; I'D BEGUN TO WORRY—
SOME VERY SHADY TYPES WERE AROUND HERE A FEW WEEKS AGO, ASKING ABOUT YOU—

ARE YOU...

...ARE YOU OKAY?
REPE CITY
ATERING
...

AH, YOU KNOW.
THE GLORBON INVASION.
FILE: FRED STUMBLEY

Th- thanks.

ANYWAY, I JUST WANTED TO LET YOU KNOW I'M FREE WHENEVER YOU NEED ME. MY BANK TELLER JOB FELL THROUGH--
AH, YES, **CREPE CITY BANK** DECLARED BANKRUPTCY. ALL OVER THE NEWS.

ha ha
WHO KNEW BANKS COULD EVEN **GO** BANKRUPT?

I GUESS WE GOT **ROBBED** ONE TOO MANY TIMES.

FRED, I'M AFRAID IT'S A **HEALTH CODE VIOLATION** FOR SOMEONE IN YOUR CONDITION TO BE HANDLING FOOD.
PLEASE, REST UP, TAKE CARE OF YOURSELF, AND CHECK BACK IN A FEW WEEKS.
BUT WITH **CONSUELO** IN THE HOSPITAL, WE'RE SHORT ON EXPERIENCED WORKERS. IS YOUR FRIEND **MARY** AVAILABLE?

I'LL--I'LL HAVE TO **ASK** HER. CONSUELO IS IN THE **HOSPITAL**?
YEAH.
MODCREPE

I THINK I SHOULD MAYBE . . . LOOK INTO GETTING YOU GUYS BETTER **HEALTH INSURANCE.**

MARY DID THIS.
Get well soon

YOU'RE NOT SERIOUS.

SHE'S IN THE BUTTERFLY GANG! DID YOU KNOW THAT? AND YOU NO TELL ME?!

YEAH, BUT...

YOU STILL TRUST HER?
NO ES BUENA GENTE.

I DON'T SPEAK SPANISH.

I WILL NOT FORGIVE AND FORGET.
CASTIGO CON VENGANZA

ONCE I HAVE **RECOVERED**...

sigh...

DID SHE DO **THAT** TO **YOU**, TOO?

NO.

I HAVEN'T SEEN HER SINCE...

GOSH, SINCE **YESTERDAY**. I THOUGHT SHE WAS WITH **YOU**.

SHOULD I CALL THE **POLICE**?

help
Sale
SOLD
raw hide
toys
YOU KWON DO IT!

I CALLED HER AND SHE JUST BABBLED NONSENSE AND HUNG UP.

CHAMPS 1997

TACOS
TACOS
Meat-o-zoid

WE HAVE our DEMANDS!
STOP RAISING SUBWAY FARES!!

GIVE US STUFF!
BADDA BADDA
WE LIKE MONEY!!
IF THESE DEMANDS ARE NOT MET...
A DISASTER BEYOND YOUR IMAGINATION WILL OCCUR!

MAYHEM!
"TRAIN"-ING DAY?
WHILE POLICE ARE WORKING TO DISCOVER THE IDENTITIES OF THE TWO "FLY GIRLS," CITIZENS ARE HOPING...

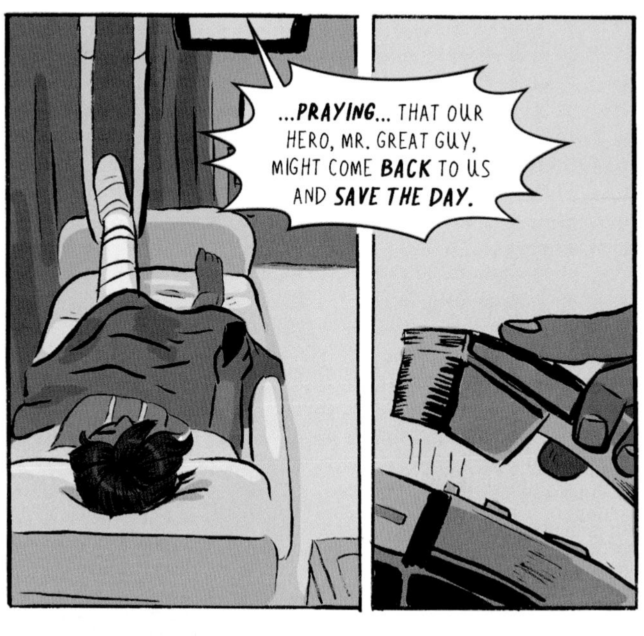
...PRAYING... THAT OUR HERO, MR. GREAT GUY, MIGHT COME BACK TO US AND SAVE THE DAY.

SEÑOR GAINS, YOU HAVE TO SAVE THESE PEOPLE. NO. IT IS NOT A NEGOTIATION.

GO.
CLICK
Beep
boop
boop

POLICE? I KNOW THIS GIRL WHO IS ROBBING THE SUBWAY. HER NAME IS...
MARY POSA.

YOU! GIVE ME YOUR STUFF!

DO I LOOK ...

GLAMOROUS ?!

EW! YOU'RE GONNA GET **EAR GERMS!**

LET'S BRING YOU TO THE COPS.
nggggh...

LET HER GO, OR...

OR I'LL SHOOT EVERY-ONE!

...GO AHEAD. WHAT DOES IT MATTER.
...oh.
HEYY...
SHIRT

HYAH!
KLONG!

THUD!

WELL,
CAN'T SAY I DIDN'T **TRY**.

OH MY GOD, THAT WAS **WAY TOO CLOSE.** YOU ALMOST BROKE MY **FACE!**
HUFF HUFF
22 St
ISH

PROBABLY WOULDA **IMPROVED** IT!

ha, ha.

THIS IS ACTUALLY PRETTY **FUN.**
Yeah!

I'M GLAD WE DIDN'T KILL YOU.
PAT PAT
huh?

HUH?!
PLONK!
!
FWOOSH
YAGH!
DANGER NO ENTRY
WHAT THE--?!
WHAT ARE YOU DOING?!
HUH?

YOU'RE ON TV--
where did they go?

THREATENING...

THERE ARE **SO** MANY THINGS **WRONG** WITH THIS.
...

I DIDN'T **WANT** TO-- IT'S MY **JOB**!

OH, LOOK WHO'S ALIVE.
MANNEQUIN.

NO... THAT'S... THAT'S SOMEONE **ELSE**.
YEAH. **OKAY**.
WHAT THE **HELL**, DUDE, YOU'RE **BLEEDING** ON ME!
s-sorry
I SHOULD JUST BRING YOU TO THE COPS **RIGHT NOW...**
WHY DON'T YOU, THEN?

MARY WOULD GET IMPLICATED.

I GOT THIS, COCO. SEE YOU LATER.

YOU GOTTA GIVE THAT STUFF BACK ...
LOOT

... TO THOSE PEOPLE.

sigh

TINA'S WAITING FOR US AT THE NEXT STOP.

YOU COULD HAVE GOTTEN YOURSELF **ARRESTED**, YOU KNOW THAT?
I GUESS COCO AND I JUST GOT **CAUGHT UP** IN THINGS. YOU KNOW. **GOOFING OFF** AND STUFF.

TH-THAT'S HOW **PSYCHOPATHS** GOOF OFF.

OH, COME ON. WE WOULDN'T HAVE **HURT** ANYONE. THAT WOULD HAVE **RAISED OUR PROFILE** TOO MUCH!

ARE YOU **FEELING** OKAY? YOU'RE **ACTING** STRANGE.

MAYBE **COCO'S** HAVING TOO MUCH OF AN **INFLUENCE** ON YOU.

TRAIN!

WROOOOOOOO
you know...

WROOOOOOOOOOO

SHE'S REALLY NOT **THAT** BAD, ONCE YOU GET TO **KNOW** HER.

ROOO

SERIOUSLY?!

well...

ngh

ASIDE FROM TRYING TO KILL YOU.

...

I'M NEVER GOING TO GET MY HALF OF THAT **LOOT**, AM I.
Hey! over here!
YEAH, POOR YOU.

Chemins de mon amour je vous cherche toujours

Chemins perdus vous n'êtes plus et vos défauts sont sourds

PS 134

SCHOOL BUS

I PACK A LUNCH.
THAT WORKS.

I THOUGHT YOU WERE NICE!!
SHLURRP I DON'T WANT TO.. IT'S MY JOB!

SHHHP
SHHHPP

THE VANDALS WERE JUST HERE.
GOOD ONE! HA HA!
SHHHP!
SPRAY IT PAINT SO!

THE BUTTERFLY GANG? YOU LITTLE PANSIES REALLY WANT TO START A TURF WAR WITH THE CHAINSAW GANG?
NYEAH! YOU'RE LIKE THE C LISTERS OF CRIME!

BUTTERFLY ZAP!
GANG
SUX

BZZT!

I... HAVE A HEART MURMUR...

huff huff

I DON'T CARE!

BUTTERFLY...

ZAP!!

BZZZT!

AHHHHHH!

YOU GUYS ARE **ANIMALS!**

THAT'S RIGHT! GO RUN HOME **TO MOMMY!**

WHY DID THAT FEEL SO **VALIDATING?**

THE BUTTERFLY DEN
NO PARKING

CREPE CITY TIMES
MR. GREAT GUY DIDN'T CARE ABOUT HOSTAGE
TOTAL JERK

AND THE EMPLOYEE OF THE WEEK IS...

MARY POSA!

WOOOO!

I AM TOTALLY FINE WITH THIS.
HIGH FIVE

OH, THESE ARE A BIT UNGAINLY. YOU CAN KEEP THEM, COCO.

THAT'S CONVENIEN STORE
MPSTER
CHEAPO PUPPIES
BUTCHER

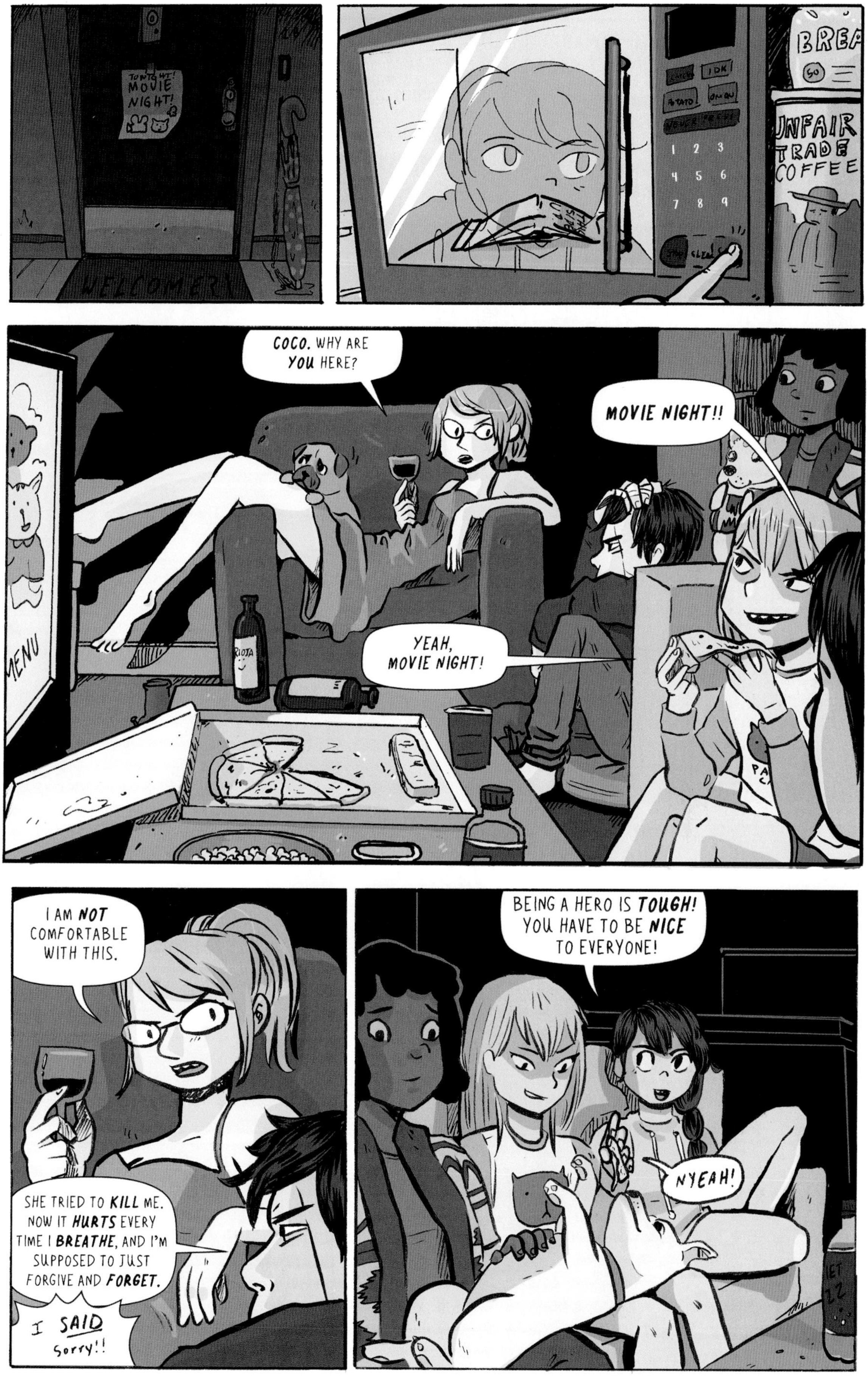

TONIGHT!
MOVIE NIGHT!
WELCOME!

UNFAIR TRADE COFFEE

COCO. WHY ARE YOU HERE?
MOVIE NIGHT!!
YEAH, MOVIE NIGHT!
RIOJA
MENU

I AM NOT COMFORTABLE WITH THIS.
SHE TRIED TO KILL ME. NOW IT HURTS EVERY TIME I BREATHE, AND I'M SUPPOSED TO JUST FORGIVE AND FORGET.
I SAID sorry!!

BEING A HERO IS TOUGH! YOU HAVE TO BE NICE TO EVERYONE!
NYEAH!

WHAT IS YOUR FAVORITE PART OF BEING A CRIMINAL?
Well...

YOU GET TO GO ON SECRET MISSIONS, WHICH ARE EXCITING... YOU DON'T HAVE TO WAKE UP EARLY IN THE MORNING... THERE'S A SENSE OF CAMARADERIE AMONG THE IDIOTS WE WORK WITH...
AND CRIME IS REALLY THE ONLY BUSINESS THAT'S BOOMING IN CREPE CITY RIGHT NOW.
Paw!

SO EXCITING!!

SAY, YOU HAVE SOME NEAT POWERS. CARROTS. WHO'D THINK THEY WOULD BE USEFUL?
THANK YOU!
I MEAN, WE COULD ALWAYS USE SOMEONE WITH REAL SUPERPOWERS ON THE TEAM.
OKAY!!

!!

CRACK!

Sue...
NO! NEVER!! OUT OF MY APARTMENT, BEAST!!
MAKE ME.
...
mua
mua

LET'S JUST WATCH THE MOVIE ALREADY.

PAJAMA CATS
THE SQUEAKQUEL
STARRING GEORGE PAUL FRANCIS

FLUSHHH
CLICK
OFF
Meow meow
I KNOW YOU DID SOMETHING TO **MARY.**
!!
WHAT ARE YOU **TALKING** ABOUT?
YOU'RE A MEDIOCRE LIAR.
I... I DON'T **CARE** WHAT YOU THINK!
WE'LL FIGURE OUT WHAT YOU DID.
Yeah, yeah. IDIOT.
SUE'S ROOM
STOMP STOMP
STOMP

FARMTOWN, WEST VIRGONIA
VRRRR

MUU

YOU'RE MAKING YOUR MOTHER **CRY!**
I DON'T **CARE!** I'VE HAD IT WITH THIS STUPID **FARM!** I'M GOING TO **ART SCHOOL!**
IF YOU WALK OUT THAT DOOR...
NOVAK

CRIME RAMPANT
FROOZIE FAKED DEATH?
GLORBON INVASION
DEATH OVER 2000
6:04
A SUPER FAMILY
THAT FOOL **BROTHER** OF YOURS HAS GOTTEN TOO BIG FOR HIS BRITCHES.

HE'S GONE AND BROKE YOUR MOTHER'S **HEART.**

HE'S **LEAVING** US.

YOU KNOW THIS MEANS YOU'RE GOING TO HAVE TO TAKE OVER THE **FARM.** YOUR MOM AND I AREN'T GETTIN' ANY **YOUNGER.**

THIS LAND HAS BEEN IN OUR FAMILY FOR **GENERATIONS.** I'VE GIVEN MY WHOLE **LIFE** TO THIS LAND.
PLANTED MY YEARS IN ITS SOIL ALONG WITH THE CORN AND GRAIN.

IF WE HAD TO SELL OUR ACRES TO **MEAT-O-ZOID,** I JUST WOULDN'T BE ABLE TO BEAR IT.
GLORBON INVASION: AN INSIDE JOB?
HAVE OUR HEROES ABANDONED US?
I UNDERSTAND, DADDY.

YOU ALWAYS WERE THE **GOOD** ONE. I'M **PROUD** OF YOU, AMELIA.
PAT PAT

I LOVE YOU.
LOVE YOU, TOO.

CLICK

DARN!
...

TICKETS
CREPE C
ONE TICKET TO CREPE CITY, PLEASE!

HENCHGIRL
VIII

Illustration by Georgeo Brooks

WE LOVE YOU
LORD CTHULU
THIS... THIS IS GREAT. WOW.
CTHULU BURGER
HEY
I LOVE YOU
I AM YOUR CB MASTER
THANKS

USING THE JEWEL OF ALETHEIA TO EXTORT VARIOUS MEMBERS OF THE CHAINSAW GANG. I THINK IT'LL YIELD IMPRESSIVE DIVIDENDS.
EVIL IDEAS

IT'LL ELEVATE THE BUTTERFLY GANG BRAND, WHILE SMEARING OUR RIVALS THROUGH THE MUD. AND WE HARDLY HAVE TO DO ANY WORK.
CTHULU BURGER
DIET
REG
SCUZZ
POISON
HI KIDS!
CTHUL

THAT'S M'STYLE!
U BURGER
EVIL PLAN

CAN I TAKE SOME OF THE CREDIT? I FEEL LIKE I'M COMPLETELY DRAINED OF DIABOLICAL SCHEMES LATELY. I'M STUCK IN THIS CLICHÉD BANK-ROBBING MINDSET.

AS LONG AS YOU CAN PROCURE THE GIANT NET... WHY NOT?

I HAVE LIKE THIRTY MORE SCHEMES.
EVIL PLAN 4: EVIL NEVER DIES
EVIL PLAN 3-D!

I THINK I STILL HAVE THE GIANT NET FROM LAST TIME.

HEY, GUYS.

HIDE THE SCHEMES!!

'SUP?

HEY, FRED! HOW'S IT GOING? SCARE ANY SMALL KIDS LATELY?

NO.

WE'RE JUST GETTING LUNCH, LIKE REGULAR CIVILIANS. WHAT ARE YOU DOING?
JUST GOT INTERVIEWED FOR A JOB HERE.
COOL.

YOU LOOK LIKE **FRANKEN-STEIN**!

WOW, GOOD ONE.

FREDENSTEIN!
CLASSIC!

WELL, **YOU** LOOK LIKE ...

OOOOOH

...A **RUDE PERSON.**
EXCUSE ME, I'M LEAVING.
FWISH!

AW, **THAT** WASN'T A GOOD BURN. SHE LOOKS LIKE A **LIZARD!**

WHAT?!! YOU LOOK LIKE... **STUPID!**

STUPID IS AN **ADJECTIVE,** STUPID.

CTHULU

MONSTER!!
It's rude to point...

FWOOP!

BUS MAP

BUS MAP
CAN YOU **BELIEVE** IT, FURRIA?!! WE'VE FINALLY **MADE** IT!

CREPE CITY! WOW! SO COOL!
BUS MAP
BUS STOP
USA'S **CRIME** CAPITAL! **FINALLY,** MY DREAMS ARE COMING **TRUE!**

LET ME GUESS. ANOTHER YOUNG CRIMINAL HOPING TO BLEED DRY THE HONEST CITIZENS OF **CREPE CITY.**
WELL, YOU'VE COME TO THE **RIGHT PLACE.**

MY PURSE!!
BUS MAP
NOPE! I'M A HERO!

ANGEL ... SPIRIT ...

MAKE UP!

UM...
bye?
HE'S GETTING AWAY!
ON IT!!
!!
W-WAIT UP!
FUNP!
KRRK!
TA
DA!

THIS WAS...
MY LAST GOOD SHIRT.
PENNY
BELLA
STOMP STOMP STOM
STOMP STOMP STOMP
CELESTIAL...
POWER!
AHHHHHH
REPENT!
4 the Police
HERE'S YOUR PURSE, CITIZEN.
WHAT A TEAM!
WE'RE NOT A--
YES WE ARE! WE'RE A TEAM.
OF COURSE NOT! ALERT THE PRESS!
I'M A BLOGGER! MIND IF I SNAP A PIC?

I'M FRED,
BY THE WAY.
AMELIA.

LOVELY CELESTIAL
ANGEL AMELIA.
...
Thanks!

DID THAT GUY
STAB YOU?!
THIS IS
NORMAL.
I'M FINE.

HOPEFULLY SOMEONE
KEPT AN EYE ON MY--

SUITCASES...

MY WORLDLY
BELONGINGS!

BUS STOP
MAP
m-maybe they're
still here ...

WELCOME TO
CREPE CITY.

DO YOU REMEMBER BEING... NOT LIKE THIS?
HUH?
HEROES weekly

DO YOU REMEMBER WHEN DOING STUFF LIKE THIS WOULD HAVE MADE YOU FEEL BAD?

I GUESS THAT'S WHAT GROWING UP IS ABOUT. YOU TOUGHEN UP.
FLIP!
HEROES

IT'S JUST...

MAYBE THEY'RE TELLING THE TRUTH. AFTER ALL, WHY WOULD THERE BE A CHEST FULL OF **MONEY** IN A **2-BEDROOM APARTMENT**?
YOU'RE NO FUN.

THE ***JEWEL OF ALETHEIA*** WOULD LET US FIND OUT RIGHT AWAY.
THAT'S no fun!!

SO WHAT MADE YOU JOIN THE **BUTTERFLY GANG**, ANYWAY?
FUNNY STORY...

lost Dog
NEED CASH?
Not afraid of getting your hands dirty?
$ Call $
suitcases suitcases
SAT tuter available
guitar lessons from Robbie
roommates
call Katie Pillar
Shred like a God

I ASSUMED THEY MEANT IT LITERALLY. LIKE **GARDENING** OR SOMETHING.
ha ha
AREN'T YOU GOING TO ASK ME WHY **I** JOINED THE BUTTERFLY GANG?

I DON'T ACTUALLY CARE. BUT IF YOU **MUST** UNLOAD...
...

FINE! NEVER MIND.

BUT IT'S A **REALLY** INTERESTING, **DRAMATIC** STORY.

I COME FROM A FAMILY OF--
HEY!

TREASURE!

I think I'm stuck...

crepebook

when you're here, you're family.

c

search

Mary Posa

edit profile

events: none
requests: none
messages: none

Sue Tanaka: LAB INSPECTION TODAY

Tina Caro: good luck

Sue: WE PASSED :D

Other Friend: blah blah science

Tina Caro: Although we've come to the end of the road, still I can't let you go. It's unnatural, you belong to me, I belong to you

Friend: omg gurl what happened

FRED STUMBLEY is now friends with **CELESTIAL ANGEL AMELIA**

Amelia wrote on Fred's wall:
The new crimefighting duo makes headlines!!! xoxoxo
LINK: ***Crepe City Safer Thanks To Celestial Angel Amelia and Friend***

I got robbed again today, lol. Whyyyyy do people keep stealing my purse? I know it's a great purse :/ but steal someone ELSE'S great purse!! GOD! How many times do I have to re-buy this purse?? (Click to continue)

ity Safer Thanks To Celestial Angel A

I got robbed again today, lol. Whyyyyy do people keep stealing my purse? I know it's a great purse :/ but steal someone ELSE'S great purse!! GOD! How many times do I have to re-buy this purse?? Anyway today my purse was rescued thanks to new crimefighting team (slash COUPLE??!! omg I totally ship them #otp #fredelia #amfred #idklolol) who basically karate'd my assailant into submission. TOTALLY COOL!!! Look how cute they are!!!

"AMELIA."
YOU DON'T KNOW WHO YOU JUST **MESSED** WITH.
CRASH
SPLATT
wruf?

WHY IS THERE A **BAGEL** ON THE GROUND?

WHY IS THERE AN OPEN THING OF **CREAM CHEESE** ON THE COUCH?

I WILL DESTROY YOUR HAPPINESS...
UHH... NEVER MIND.

AMELIA.

OOF. I THINK A GOOSE JUST WALKED OVER MY GRAVE.
...THESE MAGICAL TOOLS AREN'T TOYS, AMELIA! YOU CAN'T JUST GO AROUND GIVING THEM AWAY!

FRED AND I ARE A CRIME-FIGHTING DUO! THE FOREVER FRIENDS!

...

I'M FINE JUST USING MY MANNEQUIN POWERS. I JUST WANT TO FIGHT CRIME, I DON'T CARE ABOUT...
step step

step step
FWOOOO

...COOL GADGETS.
FWUMP

ARE YOU SURE THIS IS THE PERSON YOU WANT TO TEAM UP WITH? HE LOOKS LIKE HE'S DYING.
I'M AWFUL SORRY, FRED. FURRIA IS FROM THE OUTER WORLDS. SHE DOESN'T QUITE UNDERSTAND PEOPLE'S FEELINGS.

ANYHOW, I COULDN'T POSSIBLY USE ALL THESE DOODADS MYSELF.
AND I THINK I HAVE THE PERFECT MAGICAL ARTIFACTS FOR YOU.

THIS SHROUD OF LAZARUS WILL HEAL YOUR BODILY AILMENTS--

AS LONG AS YOU'RE ...

OH ... MY GOD... AHHHHHH. I FORGOT WHAT IT FEELS LIKE TO NOT HURT EVERYWHERE.
PLOMP!
...WEARING IT.

AND THIS CLOCK, IT'S A MAGIC CLOCK.

NOT THE TIMEKEEPER! THAT OBJECT IS INTENDED FOR YOUR RIGHT-HAND OFFICER, THE TIME BARON!!!
FRED CAN BE THE TIME BARON.

BUT HE ISN'T THE TIME BARON! IT ISN'T HIS DESTINY!
I'M FINE WITH JUST THE BLANKET.

DESTINY, SHMESTINY. YOU DIDN'T THINK I WAS DESTINED TO BE THE CELESTIAL ANGEL, AND HERE I AM!
VERY WELL.

SO HOW DOES THIS WORK?

THWOSHH

CRAKK!
I CAN PAY FOR THAT.

IS... IS THIS SUPPOSED TO HAPPEN?
CHK CHK CHK CHK

?!
TESTING, TESTIN
CHK CHK

CHK CHK CHK
IS THIS THING ON?

WHOA... IT'S NEVER DONE THAT BEFORE! FURRIA, WHAT DOES IT MEAN?
THE FABLED MESSAGES FROM BEYOND...
MAYBE IT IS YOUR DESTINY TO BE THE TIME BARON, FRED.

CHK CHK CHKKKK
TRANSMISSION END.
BEWARE THE CATACLYSM!!

WHAT?!! WHAT'S THE CATACLYSM?

NO...
NO...

FRED DUMPED YOU?

WE WEREN'T ACTUALLY GOING OUT.
AFTER YOU LITERALLY PUT HIM BACK TOGETHER?!! NOW HE'S WITH SOME OTHER GIRL?!!!
MISSING
Sniff

WHY BUY THE COW WHEN... YOU...
SAVE AN EGG

THANKS. NICE TO KNOW YOU THINK OF ME AS A COW.
YOU'RE A BEAUTIFUL, STRONG COW. A COW WHO DOESN'T NEED FRED, OR ANY OTHER MAN.

YOU WANT TO HELP ME GET SOME VENGEANCE? MAYBE WE COULD USE SOME OF THOSE... CREEPY CARROT DUDES...
YOU'LL HAVE AN ARMY OF THEM.

HEY!!
Donuts

STOP TAKING ADVANTAGE OF TINA'S DELICATE EMOTIONAL STATE.

PLAN B, THEN.

FOOLISH GAMES
JEWEL STORE
WEEEE
P.S. 180
STOP RACIAL PROFILING!
SUPPORT LOCAL FARMERS! NO GMOS!
CCPD
I FOUND YOUR FRISBEE!
PUPPY MILLS ARE INHUMANE!
PAY YOUR DARN TAXES!
TAX FRAUD
CHEAPO PUPPIES
FANCYMOBILE
Scratch
FWOOo

ANOTHER CRIME PREVENTED!
FWIP FWIP!

ANGEL AMELIA!
?

MY NERMERSERS!
OW! HEY!

IT'S CELESTIAL ANGEL AMELIA.
WELL, THAT'S REDUNDANT.

HELP!

I'VE GOT A MIND TO TEACH YOU A LESSON ABOUT PERSONAL BOUNDARIES... BUT I'M A CRIME FIGHTER, NOT A STREET FIGHTER. AND I'VE GOT SOME CRIMES TO FIGHT.
ALL RIGHT, AMELIA... YOU DON'T WANT TO FIGHT? THAT WORKS FOR ME.

Wh- what's WRONG with me?
!

YOU'RE BURNING UP!

DID YOU KNOW THAT MONARCH BUTTERFLIES ARE POISONOUS?

NEITHER DID I, UNTIL I GOOGLED "POISONOUS BUTTERFLIES." IT'S A THING.
AND WHEN THE POISON IS DISTILLED, IT CAN BE... VERY LETHAL.
P-POISON? I'M AN ANGEL OF PURITY! Y-YOUR POISON CAN'T...

FLICKKK...
USE YOUR DIVINITY STICK!
Angel...

H-healing...

POWER!

LIKE I SAID... YOUR POISON CAN'T HURT ME.
...

HYUGH!
YOU SHOULD ...
... "LEAF" this city!!
ZONK!
YOU'RE A REAL **THORN** IN MY SIDE, WHOEVER YOU ARE.
Heh. Haha haha. Um ...
... YOU NEED TO **BRANCH OUT!**
SHONK!
UGH! STUPID **BUSH!**
FSHH
BUTTERFLY **ZAP!!**

BLOOSHK!
CELESTIAL POWER!
GOD DAMMIT! LET ME HURT YOU!
huff huff
huff huff
YOU HAVEN'T GOT THE SENSE GOD GAVE A GOOSE.
OBVIOUSLY I'M SMARTER THAN A GOOSE.
WH-WHO ARE YOU TO CALL ME DUMB?
YOU CAN'T BEAT ME.
You Should Know... I'm actually pretty Smart...
CELESTIAL POWER!
ZAP
REVEEEEEEEENGE!

CTHULU BU

THAT'S RIGHT, EMPTY THE **REGISTERS**!

AND, UH, A VALUE CTHULU BURGER WITH **EXTRA CTHULU MAYO!**

YOU WANT **FRIES** WITH THAT?
CTHULU BURG

HEY!

BREAKFAST TENTACLES (till 11) $1.00
DRINKS: SCUZZ, EVIL SCUZZ, THE NAMELESS MIST, INK JUICE, SALT WATER, MALK
COMBO SPECIAL: YOU GIVE US MONEY AND WORSHIP CTHULU WHAT A DEAL!
EVERYONE GET DOWN! I'VE GOT THIS!

BAM!

OH MY GOD... NOW **THAT'S** COMPANY DEDICATION! YOU'RE GETTING A **PROMOTION!** $8.50 AN HOUR, HOW'S ABOUT **THAT?**

WHY CAN'T YOU GUYS BE MORE LIKE ***FRED?!***

I'M NOT IN IT FOR THE GLORY, OR THE EXTRA DOLLAR AN HOUR.

I WOULD HAVE DONE IT EVEN **WITHOUT** THE **SHROUD OF LAZARUS'S** PROTECTION. ...DID THAT SOUND SELF-AGGRANDIZING?

ALL PROCEEDS GO TO LORD CTHULU

Now with Dipping ooze!

BREAKFAST TENTACLES (til 11) $1.00

QUENCH THE THIRSTS OF A THOUSAND HORDES!! DRINKS: SCUZZ, EVIL SCUZZ, THE NAMELESS MIST, INK JUICE, SALT WATER, MALK

OLD ONES GET 20% DISCOUNT!

WIN A TRIP TO R'LYEH! *LIMITED TIME OFFER.*

AUTOGRAPHS

...WHO CARES, NO ONE CAN HEAR WHAT I'M THINKING. ***YEAH.***

BIG TOUGH HERO. LOOK AT ALL THESE **GIRLS** WHO ARE SO **IMPRESSED** BY ME.

HENCHGIRL

KRISTEN GUDSNUK

READ THE SMASH HIT MEMOIR THAT'S **SUPER** INTERESTING!

"A... near-perfect example of... what... to do... when writing... a... book.... Great." --BB Bowb, ***The AV Clob***

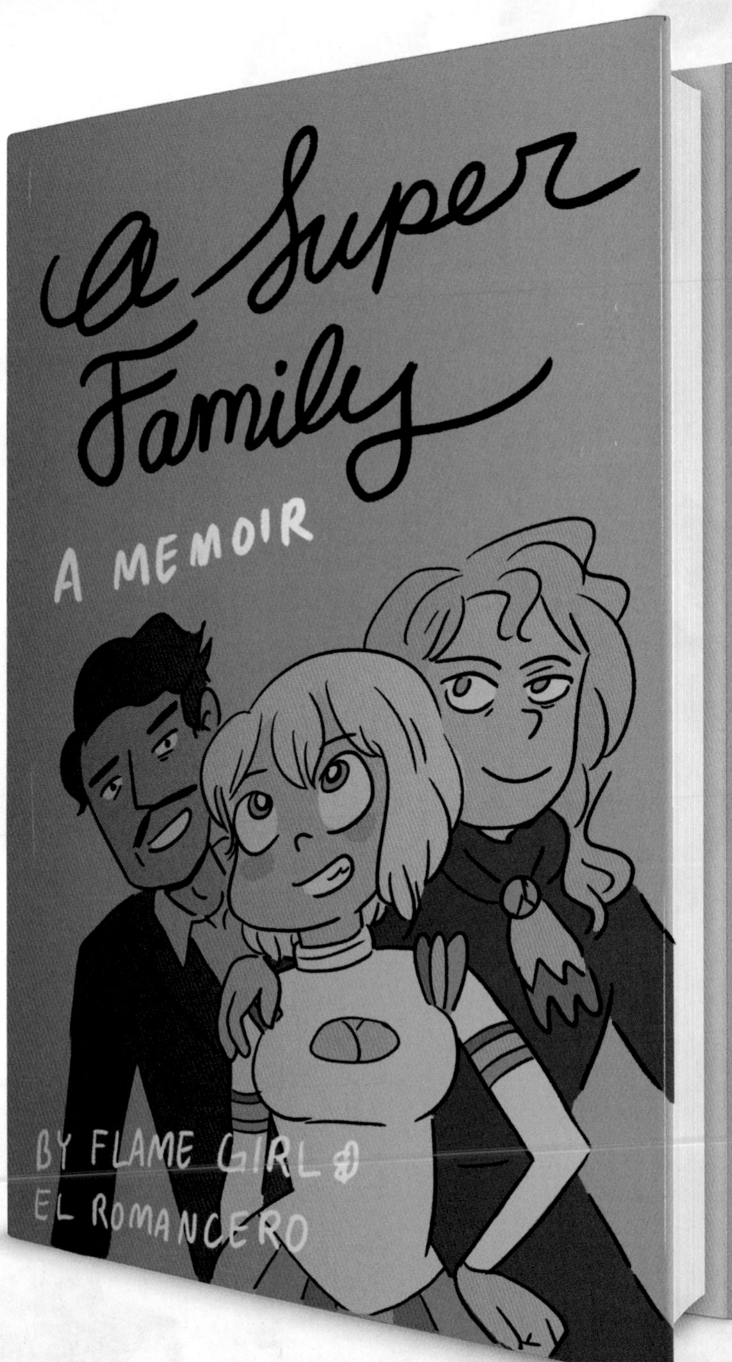

"I've never read a book before, but this one feels nice in my hands!"
--Jerty

"Thizz izz a book. Okay, you've got your blurb, leave me to my *hic* mizzery. [*Unintelligible*]"
--Mr. Great Guy

"A fascinating look into my nemeses' strategies and mindset! Three and a half stars."
--The Pointed Rogue

10% of proceeds go to the Glorbon Relief Fund!

OUT
...JUST THINK! MY NAME ON THE DOOR, NO MORE LIFE OF CRIME.
ISN'T THAT AMAZING?
NO PARKI

SO YOU'RE GOING STRAIGHT.

I KNOW YOU'RE ALWAYS SAYING YOU WANT TO QUIT THE BUTTERFLY GANG... WOULD YOU WANT TO WORK WITH ME? IT'D BE A REAL JOB! YOU CAN EVEN PAY YOUR TAXES!
AW MAN, TAXES SOUND REALLY TEMPTING, BUT...

IN CONCLUSION, IF WE ROB THE VICTORIAN DOLL FACTORY, WE WILL NOT ONLY WALK AWAY WITH A TREASURE TROVE OF VALUABLES, BUT ALSO SOME OF THE LOVELIEST COLLECTOR'S ITEMS KNOWN TO MAN. CRINOLINE, LACE, PAINTED SMILES, PORCELAIN SKIN, EYES THAT ROLL BACK--
DOLLS
The History of Dolls
Dolls: Secretly Alive?
Madame Alexander: An Oral History

VICTORIAN DOLLS! RECAPTURE YOUR CHILDHOOD... AND SOME FUN MONEY.
UH... ANYONE ELSE HAVE A DIABOLICAL SCHEME YOU'D LIKE TO PRESENT?

THIS ISN'T A SCHEME, MORE OF AN ANNOUNCEMENT. I'M OPENING A PRIVATE INVESTIGATION BUSINESS NEXT MONTH! PUTTING ALL THE INVALUABLE SKILLS I'VE LEARNED HERE TO GOOD USE. SO UNFORTUNATELY, MONSIEUR B, THIS IS MY TWO WEEKS' NOTICE.
BUT IF ANYONE HAS SOMETHING THEY WANT INVESTIGATED--

WHAT?! YOU CAN'T QUIT.
BUT I PUT A DOWN PAYMENT ON THE OFFICE ALREADY...
NO, LIKE, NO ONE CAN QUIT THE BUTTERFLY GANG. IT'S A GANG.

YOU'RE IN IT FOR **LIFE.** **RIGHT,** LARRY?

nod

WHY WOULD YOU WANT AN **EMPLOYEE** WHO DOESN'T WANT TO **WORK** FOR YOU?

WHEN YOU **JOIN,** YOU MAKE AN **OATH**--

THEY'RE NOT GOING TO **TRY HARD**, OBVIOUSLY THEY WON'T BE **LOYAL** IF YOU'RE USING **COERCION...**

ENOUGH!

SPROING!

ZAP!

JESUS CHRIST, WOULD YOU SHUT UP ALREADY??!

I... I REALLY FEEL STRONGLY...

WE ALL GET IT. YOUR POINT HAS BEEN MADE. ASSESS THE CURRENT ENVIRONMENT, AND HOW YOUR IDIOTIC PRATTLE IS NEGATIVELY AFFECTING IT.
YOU'RE SUPPOSED TO BE MY FRIEND.

FRIENDS LISTEN TO EACH OTHER'S TRAGIC BACKSTORIES.
YOUR STUPID BACKSTORY IS BORING!
WAHHH

SLAM!

WHAT A WEIRDO!

hic
THEY'RE PROBABLY IN THERE... TALKING ABOUT ME...

well...
shift

IS EVERYTHING OKAY?

HERE'S SOMETHING TO TALK ABOUT.
BEEP!
CHKK!
STOP SPYING ON ME, FRED!!!

FRED

Messages

Are you around? I want to talk

are you spying on me?!!

a. that is an invasion of your privacy and b. I don't really go mannequin anymore

BUT AREN'T YOU **MANNEQUIN**? ISN'T THAT, LIKE, YOUR **IDENTITY**?

WELL, IT'S NOT TOO GREAT FOR MY HEALTH. SO NOT ANYMORE. ACTUALLY, NOW I'M THE **TIME BARON**.

BUT... MANNEQUIN WAS **COOL**...

YOU... YOU KNOW THAT GIRL **AMELIA**? WE'VE BEEN TEAMING UP...

YOUR UNDERAGE **GIRLFRIEND**?

OH, I **KNOW** HER.

MAYBE IT'S BECAUSE YOU'RE ALL BUDDY-BUDDY WITH COCO ALL OF A SUDDEN.
I DON'T... THINK I NEED HELP. I'M KINDA BROKE, BUT OTHER THAN THAT... NOT MUCH.

I MEAN, I FEEL LIKE I HATE EVERYONE, NOT TO BE ALL TEEN ANGSTY.
THAT IS PRETTY TEEN ANGSTY.
FSK

EVERYONE AT WORK THINKS I'M DUMB!

WELL, MAYBE THEY'RE BURNING ALIVE RIGHT NOW.

YEAH.

WAIT, WHAT?

OH, IT'S... IT'S AN EXPRESSION.
ruf.

SAY... WHATEVER HAPPENED THAT NIGHT YOU STOLE THE JEWEL OF ALETHEIA?
HUH? WHY DOES EVERYONE KEEP ASKING ME ABOUT THAT? AND HOW DO YOU EVEN KNOW ABOUT IT?
YOU... YOU TOLD ME ABOUT IT, REMEMBER?

I DUNNO. STOLE THE JEWEL, THEN I WENT ON A BENDER AND BEAT THE TAR OUT OF CONSUELO.
WHY DID YOU DO THAT??

SHE STARTED IT. SHE KICKED ME IN THE FACE AND BROKE MY GOGGLES.
sigh...
DING!
pat
pat
shh

?

CHK, CHK CHK
AMELIA SUX

HAH!
LOOKS LIKE AMELIA'S NOT SO GREAT AFTER ALL!
SHE DOES SEEM A LITTLE TOO GOOD TO--
DING!

"THAT MESSAGE WAS SENT IN ERROR"
PLEASE DISREGARD

Huh.

WOW, THIS TIMEKEEPER THING IS REALLY NEAT. WHAT DOES THIS BUTTON--

I THINK THAT'S ENOUGH MONKEYING AROUND WITH MAGICAL ARTIFACTS.
well why do YOU get to monkey around

CREPE CITY
NOVEMBER 5
we're trying, okay?
GALA TO CELEBRATE FLAME GIRL AND EL ROM
CONTRIBUTIONS TO PEACE
TONIGHT AT GAINS TOWER BALLROOM
"This is gonna RULE!" — Anonymous Source
By BLOOB Pheremony
wow I'm excited!
Just, like, they're so great! El Romancero will be rockin' a 'stache, of course, and muttering incantations. We're not even mad they were AWOL in the Glorbon Invasion!! All is forgiven. Unlike Mr. Great Guy, who has not been seen since his controversial "Go ahead and kill the hostages" debacle.
courtesy of ©1990
GUNPOWDER RELEASED F
PRISON
NBD

IS **FRED** DRAGGING YOU ALONG TO THAT?
NAH. I THINK **ONE** AWKWARD FAMILY DINNER WAS ENOUGH FOR HIM.
IS **PAIGE** GONNA BE IN THE CITY? MAYBE SHE CAN COME OVER AFTERWARD.
GT

YEAH... I SHOULD INVITE HER. I'M SURE SHE'D **LOVE** THIS DUMP.

OH, COME ON. SHE'S YOUR **SISTER**. SHE'S NOT GOING TO JUDGE OUR CHARMINGLY SHITTY **APARTMENT**.
I'LL SEE IF I RUN INTO HER. MAYBE SHE CAN GIVE ME SOME **MONEY**.

GAINS TOWERS

CLK
BEST HEROES
CLK
CLK

YOU'RE NOT ON THE LIST.
YEAH, I'M ACTUALLY FLAME GIRL AND EL ROMANCERO'S **DAUGHTER**, SO...

YOU'RE NOT PHOTO-GIRL.

THEIR **OTHER** DAUGHTER!

LISTEN, LADY, I READ **A SUPER FAMILY** LIKE **FIVE** TIMES. AND YOU WERE **NOT** IN THAT BOOK.
THAT'S--THAT'S BECAUSE...

THE **EDITORS...**

SAVE IT, LADY.

sigh
WANTED

FOR SUBWAY ROBBERY
WANTE
stupid... editors...

NO RECYCLABLES
GARBAGE

NO RECYCLABLES
GARBAGE

IZZA

mutter mutter
THANKS!

FLAME RETARDANT, **CHECK.** VOCAL INTERRUPTERS, **CHECK.**
PHOTO-GIRL IS TIED UP BATTLING **BUZZSAW** DOWNTOWN. AND BUZZ HAS GOT **PLENTY** OF **TIME CRYSTALS.**
AND... THE HALL IS NICE AND **RIGGED.** THIS SHOULD BE **FUN.**
NO RECYCLABLES
GARBAGE

WAS THAT-- THAT WAS TOTALLY **GUNPOWDER.** NOT TOO **SUBTLE**, DUDE.

...TIME AND TIME AGAIN, **FLAME GIRL** AND **EL ROMANCERO** HAVE COME TO THIS COUNTRY'S AID, WHETHER IN THE GREAT BATTLE OF **NEW FORK CITY**, OR IN OUR **OWN** CITY'S SKIRMISHES.
ALTHOUGH AN INTERGALACTIC BATTLE OF THEIR **OWN** KEPT THESE HEROES FROM FIGHTING THE GLORBON INVASION, THEIR GENEROUS RELIEF DONATION OF TEN PERCENT OF THE ROYALTIES FROM **A SUPER FAMILY** WILL HELP **CREPE CITY** GET BACK ON OUR FEET AGAIN.

SO JOIN ME IN RAISING A **TOAST** TO--
MAYOR

FSS
FSS

FWISH
!!

IT'S GUNPOWDER!

BIG, TOUGH **HEROES.**
MAYOR

YOU WEREN'T SO HEROIC BACK IN **COLLEGE**, WERE YOU, **FLAME GIRL**? WHEN YOU SAID NO WHEN I ASKED IF YOU WOULD BE MY **LAB PARTNER** IN **CHEMISTRY**. WHICH IS IRONIC BECAUSE, I'LL HAVE YOU KNOW, I'M ACTUALLY **AMAZING** AT CHEMISTRY. I'VE CRAFTED MY ENTIRE **PERSONA** AROUND IT.
WHY COULDN'T YOU GIVE ME YOUR ATTENTION? WAS I NOT **IMPRESSIVE** ENOUGH? I COULD HAVE **HELPED** YOU!
BUT YOU NEVER CARED.

I WAS JUST ANOTHER **MOTH** TO YOUR **FLAME...**

YOU MUST NOT BE **THAT** GREAT OF A CHEMIST. YOU KNOW WHAT HAPPENS WHEN YOU COMBINE **FIRE** AND **GUNPOWDER**, DON'T YOU?

SPEEK-NO-MORE™
MRPH MRPH MRPH!

YOUR SPELLS WON'T HELP YOU NOW!

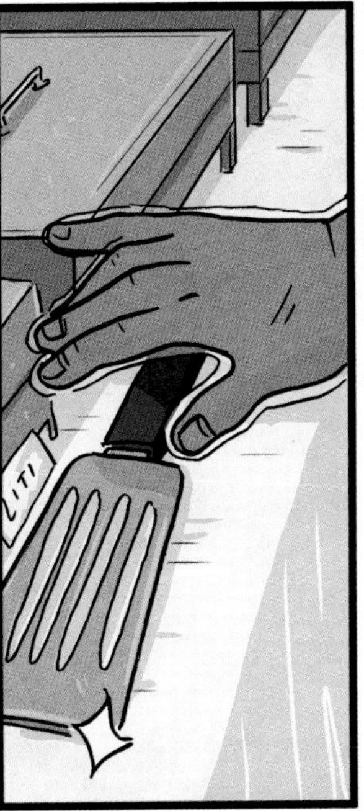

SHNG!
THIS PLACE IS RIGGED WITH EXPLOSIVES! NOBODY MOVE!

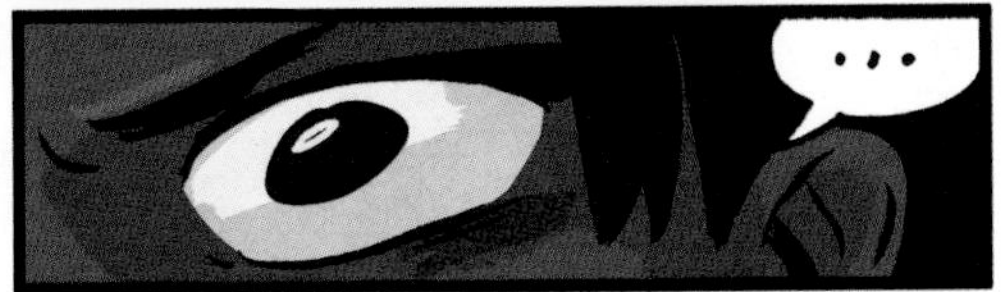

...

Where's PHOTO-GIRL?!
TOO BAD YOUR **DAUGHTER** ISN'T HERE TO SAVE YOU. LOOKS LIKE **TIME**... IS NOT ON YOUR SIDE.

THINK AGAIN!!
I THINK I WENT TO SCHOOL WITH THAT GIRL.
MARY! YOU'RE GONNA GET HURT! WHAT ARE YOU DOING HERE?!!

JUST SAVING YOU.

WHO THE HELL ARE YOU?
I'M THEIR OTHER DAUGHTER.

THERE'S... THERE'S MORE OF YOU?! STAY BACK! STAY BACK OR THIS LADY GETS IT!
I'M SURE SHE DESERVES IT SOMEWHAT.
WH-WHAT? WHAT DID I EVER--
I SAID STAY BACK!!
SHWIN
THUD
gurg...
SHE'S DEAD.
DOC
YOU MIGHT WANT TO MOVE, DOC.

ngh...

SINCE YOU LIKE **GUNPOWDER** SO MUCH...
FSSSS

YOU'RE GOING OUT WITH A **BANG!**

BUTTERFLY...

ZAP!!

BOOM
plip!

WELL, LOOKS LIKE EVERYONE'S **SAFE** NOW! ENJOY THE REST OF YOUR **GALA**!

FREEZE!

SHK SHK

OH, C'MON. I JUST **SAVED** THE **DAY**!

SHK SHK

...

THUDDD

GUESS WE'RE DOING THIS THE **HARD** WAY.

BUTTERFLY ZAP!
hyuk!
BZZZ
BUTTERFLY ZAP!
BZZZ
SWAT
BZZZ
BZZZ
SO HEAVY
SWAT

Venganza...
EXIT

YOU HAVE THE RIGHT TO REMAIN... UH... QUIET.

YES, INDEED, I AM **FLAME GIRL** AND **EL ROMANCERO'S** DAUGHTER. BEST-KEPT SECRET IN TOWN.
Snap
Snap
I DEFUSED **LOS EXPLOSIVOS.**
SWAT

EXIT
BAM!
WHERE'S GUNPOWDER?!

LOOK AROUND! HE'S **EVERYWHERE!**
omg... photo-Girl...
Snap
Snap

MARY?

WHAT... WHAT HAVE YOU DONE?!
JUST TRYING MY HAND AT THE **FAMILY BUSINESS.**
She looked at me...
sin comentarios

POSA, MARY
24601

POSA, MARY
24601
CREPE CITY PENITENTIARY

...I THOUGHT THEY MEANT **GARDENING** OR SOMETHING!

HEY MAN, THIS WAS ALL A **MISUNDERSTANDING**. DO YOU THINK--
YOU CAN KEEP TELLING YOUR ***HILARIOUS ANECDOTES*** ALL YOU WANT, BUT I'M NOT GONNA JUST LET YOU *GO*.

YOU **KILLED** A GUY. ON **NATIONAL TV.**

YOU'RE GOING **UPSTATE.**
HOT Sexy babes who love cops
AWOOGA!

VROooo
POLICE
Wel come to Crepe City
Please love us!

gnaw gnaw

EW! CUT THAT OUT!
COP

OH GOD...
I REALLY
SCREWED UP.

WHAT THE HELL IS
WRONG WITH ME?

UM...
ARE YOU REALLY FLAME GIRL
AND EL ROMANCERO'S KID?
CC PD
COP

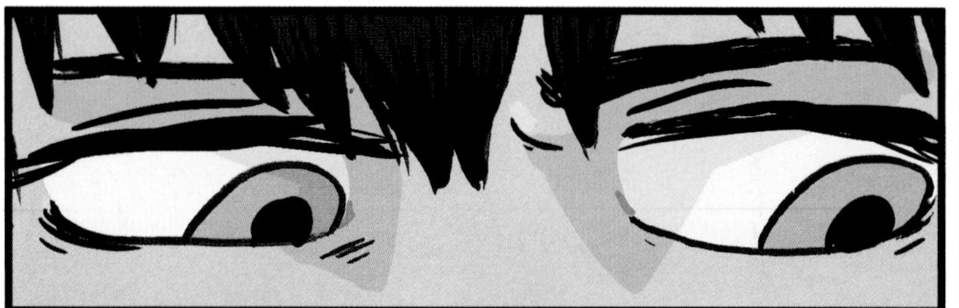

WHAT ARE THEY LIKE?

THEY TOTALLY...

SUCK.
NOW LEAVING CREPE CITY
wait! Come back! was it something we said?!

PG132
POLICE
POLICE
huh?!

FWOOOOOO
poof

UH. **THANKS?** WHO ARE YOU?

SO...

...

WHAT AM I SUPPOSED TO DO **NOW**?

POOF!

UH... **BYE?**
F W O O O O O

nghh...

ugh...
THUMP.

HAIR BAG
FWAP!

WELCOME TO CREPE CITY
oh god we missed you

HENCHGIRL
Please!
NO
TRESPASSING
CONDEMNED
DANGER
CHAINSAW
GANG

CCPD COP
HA HA HA
COP
YOU KNOW WHERE THE BATHROOM IS?
AW MAN, I GOTTA GO TOO. IT'S OVER HERE, C'MON.
CREEEE

THAT'S LIFE!
FWOOSH

THAT'S LIFE!
WORTH IT
nggg...
YANK

OLD JUNK

CIVIL WAR RE ENACT MENT

Diary
A SUPER FAMILY
JOURNAL 1995
CREPIPEDIA GIZMO
OLD JUNK

CIVIL WAR RE ENACT MENT
WHAT ARE YOU DOING?

JUST GATHERING **EVIDENCE.** LOOKS LIKE SHE WAS MAYBE PLANNING TO RUN ANYWAY-- I FOUND THIS SUITCASE IN HER CLOSET, FULL OF STUFF.
A **GETAWAY BAG**, AS I'D CALL IT.
DO YOU KNOW WHERE THE **EVIDENCE BAGS** ARE?
FWISHH
YOU DIDN'T HEAR? **REALLY? CUTBACKS.** NO MORE EVIDENCE BAGS.

WE HAVE SOME **SANDWICH** BAGS, THOUGH...
ZOPLICK™

OH, DUH. SORRY, I WAS ON SABBATICAL FOR A FEW MONTHS. WELL--

I'LL TRY NOT TO **CONTAMINATE** THE **EVIDENCE...**
HA
HA
HA
HA
HA
"EVIDENCE"

man, she's the best
run us through the story once more, girls...

I HAVE NO IDEA WHERE SHE'D GO! **REALLY!**
WE THOUGHT SHE WORKED AS A **CATERER.** WE HAD NO IDEA...
scribble
"EVIDEN

...ABOUT HER LIFE OF CRIME.
WE'RE VERY WORRIED ABOUT HER. SOMETHING'S CLEARLY **WRONG.**
scribble

She NEEDS HELP!!
YOU need help.
POLICE LINE
meep!

sigh...
98

I need help.
MR. FLV's all nite Coughee shop
OPEN

FRED?

...
COP
COP

CIVIL WAR
OKAY, NEVER MIND.

Ding Ding

WHAP!

COCO! IT'S ME!
2C
MARY?
WHAT ARE YOU DOING HERE? AND... WHY ARE YOU DRESSED AS A **COP?**
SLAM

I'M TOTALLY SCREWED. I RUINED MY LIFE.

I... I CAN FIX THIS, THOUGH.

I TOOK THIS JACKET WHEN I ESCAPED. HOW I ESCAPED, I STILL DON'T UNDERSTAND.
SO YOU ESCAPED FROM AN ARMORED VAN... AND DON'T KNOW HOW?
YEAH, I NEED... TIME... TO PROCESS THAT.
TURTLE
COP

I SAW WHAT HAPPENED ON TV. THAT WAS REALLY AWESOME HOW YOU EXPLODED THAT GUY. YOU'VE EVEN GOT AN INTERNET FAN BASE NOW.
f-fanbase?!
TURTLE RECALL

MAINLY UPSKIRT ENTHUSIASTS...
TURTLE RECALL

EH, I'LL TAKE WHAT I CAN GET.
BUT SOME PEOPLE WHO ADMIRE YOUR VIGILANTISM.
ANYWAY, I'LL LET YOU STAY HERE.

BUT FIRST...
TURTLE RECALL

TIK

TOK

...AND THAT'S HOW I GOT ROPED INTO THIS WHOLE LIFE-OF-CRIME BUSINESS.
GREAT STORY. YOU KNOW, VERY TRAGIC.
RIGHT??! I KEEP THINKING IT'D MAKE A GREAT MOVIE OR SOMETHING.
LIFE JOURNAL

IS THAT...

IS THAT A **BABY GLORBON?!!**
TURTLE RECALL

REMEMBER WHEN MONSIEUR B MADE A DEAL WITH THE **GLORBONS**? IT WAS KINDA... A **FOREIGN EXCHANGE** SORTA THING.
TURTLE RECALL

DID WE EXCHANGE SOMEONE?
OH YEAH, ONE OF KATIE PILLAR'S COUSINS. I'M SURE HE OR SHE IS FINE.

ONE SEC.
M. BUTTER FLY

HELLO? UM, MARY'S NOT HERE, WHY WOULD SHE BE HERE.
TURTLE RECALL

SHE'S FIRED FROM THE **BUTTERFLY GANG?** EH, YOU KNOW MY THOUGHTS ON THE SUBJECT.

I WANTED TO DUMP HER BODY IN THE RIVER, REMEMBER?
YOU... YOU **DID?!**

REALLY, SHE'S NOT HERE. THAT WAS THE TV.
Shh!

I GUESS I'M...
I UNDERSTAND. OKAY. BYE.
COP

FIRED FROM THE BUTTERFLY GANG?

YOUR POWERS OF DEDUCTION ARE ASTOUNDING.
TURTLE RECALL

I THOUGHT NO ONE CAN LEAVE THE BUTTERFLY GANG.
I GUESS HE'S MAKING AN EXCEPTION FOR YOU.
roof?
YOU "RAISED OUR PROFILE TOO MUCH." ALSO YOU "STOLE THE MONARCH SCEPTER," WHICH MONSIEUR BUTTERFLY WANTS BACK.

MORE LIKE MONSIEUR BUTTFACE. WELL, HE'S NOT GETTING THE MONARCH SCEPTER BACK. CONSIDER IT MY SEVERANCE.

DO YOU THINK HE'LL PUT A HIT OUT ON ME? SHOULD I KILL HIM?
THEN I'D BE UNEMPLOYED! DON'T!!

IF HE PUTS A HIT ON YOU, TRUST ME, I'LL BE THE FIRST TO KNOW.
TURTLE RECALL

...AND THEN I CAN KILL HIM. COME ON, YOU CAN BE MADAME BUTTERFLY!
I DO LIKE THE SOUND OF THAT.
COP

HAH, I BET LARRY'S THE NEXT ONE TO BLOW SOME GUY UP AT A FANCY EVENT.

WHATEVER, YOU SAY YOU CAN FIX IT, RIGHT?
EVIL PLAN 13: NO OTHER ALTERNATIVE By Mary Pose
IT'S A PRETTY COMPLICATED EVIL PLAN.
"EVIDENCE"

EVIL PLAN 13: NO OTHER ALTERNATIVE
By Mary Pose

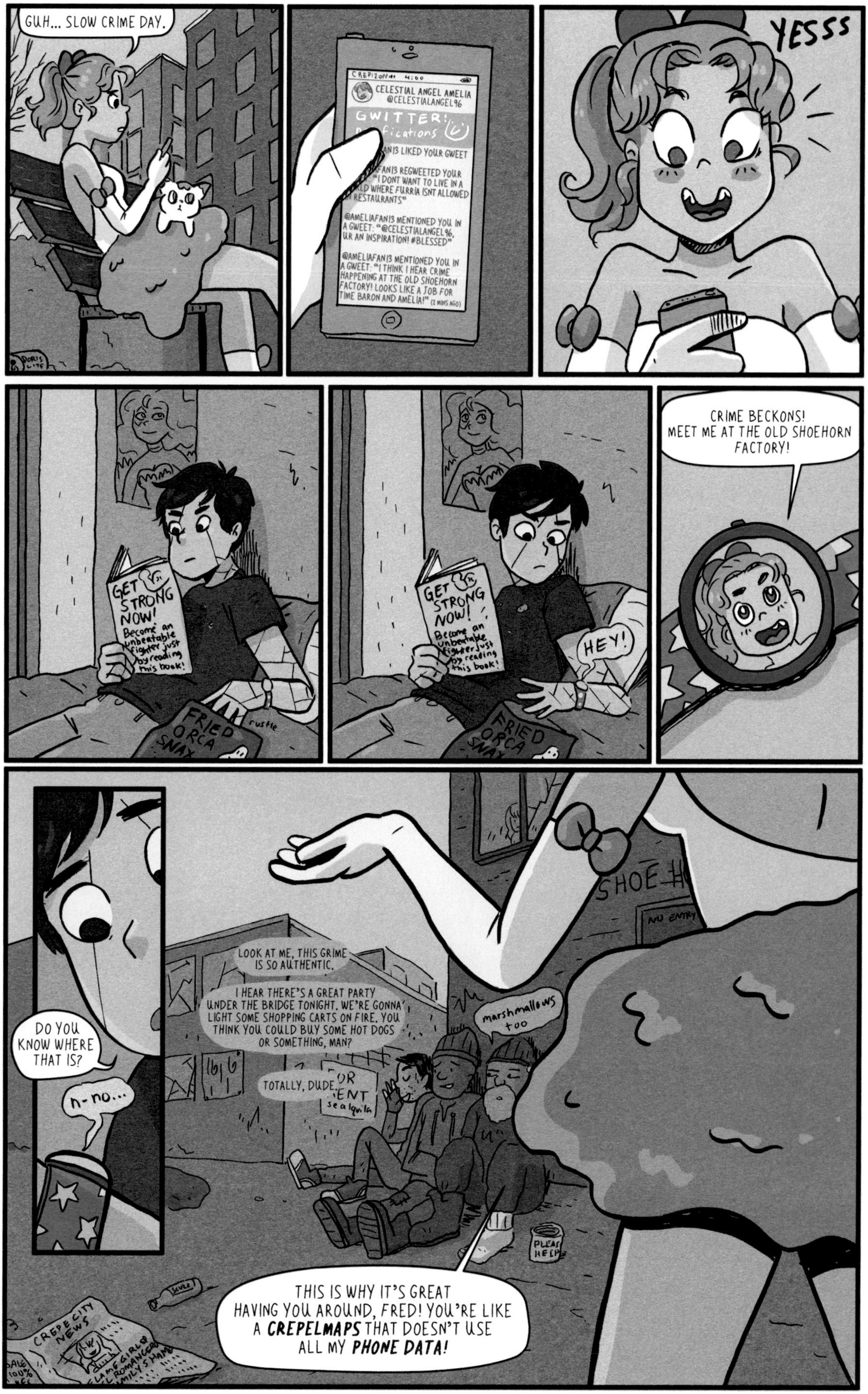

DO YOU KNOW WHERE THAT IS?

n-no...

LOOK AT ME, THIS GRIME IS SO AUTHENTIC.

I HEAR THERE'S A GREAT PARTY UNDER THE BRIDGE TONIGHT. WE'RE GONNA LIGHT SOME SHOPPING CARTS ON FIRE. YOU THINK YOU COULD BUY SOME HOT DOGS OR SOMETHING, MAN?

marshmallows too

TOTALLY, DUDE.

SHOE H

NO ENTRY

OR ENT sealquila

PLEASE HELP

CREPE CITY NEWS

THIS IS WHY IT'S GREAT HAVING YOU AROUND, FRED! YOU'RE LIKE A **CREPELMAPS** THAT DOESN'T USE ALL MY ***PHONE DATA!***

I HATE BOTH OF THEM. DESERVE EACH OTHER. **GGGHGHGHG.**
...AMONG MANY OTHER VALIANT QUALITIES, OF COURSE.

YOU NEED TO END YOUR OBSESSION WITH THIS **FRED** GUY.

I'M NOT OBSESSED! I DON'T CARE ABOUT HIM **AT ALL!!**

OKAY, ON THE COUNT OF THREE-- ONE, TWO--

HELP!!
OH MY **GOSH!**

NO GRAFITTI
CLOMP
CLOMP

SPLASH
?!

M-Mary?
YANK

heh!

WHA--
FSSSSS
IT'S **MAGIC INHIBITOR SERUM!**
CRACK!

NOOOO! THE DIVINITY STICK!!!

NICE TRY! I HAVE LIKE SIX MORE TRANSFORMATION STICKS!

...AT HOME.
THE **DIVINITY STICK** IS **IRREPLACEABLE,** AMELIA!

FWSHH

CLANK

CRASH!

MARY! COCO! WH-WHAT ARE YOU DOING?!

LET ME OUT!

FRED! YOU KNOW THIS... THIS **JERK?**

CLANG

CLANG

YEAH...

I SAW ON TV! YOU **KILLED** A GUY! YOU'RE **WICKED!**
WHAT... IS WRONG...
sliide

WOW, THIS THING... OOH.
WITH YOU...
Grope

WHAT CAN I SAY. YOU REALLY DO KNOW HOW TO DEVISE AN EVIL PLAN.
HA!

DO YOU EVEN... KNOW HOW THAT THING WORKS?

OH, YOUR LITTLE PAL AMELIA IS AN AVID BLOGGER. HER FUMBLR IS VERY... INFORMATIVE.

AMELIA! YOU DISCLOSED THE MAGICAL SECRETS OF THE TIMEKEEPER ON THE INTERNET?!!
well...
slap!

AND GUESS WHAT? AMELIAFAN13 IS ME.

NO!!!

YOUR FAN BASE... IS NONEXISTENT!
YOU TRULY ARE EVIL...
HA HA HA!

YOU KNOW WHERE I SCREWED UP? BECOMING A CRIMINAL.

DUH.

AS FUN AS IT IS TO TERRORIZE THE MASSES, THERE'S A REASON THE SOCIAL CONTRACT EXISTS. SUCCESSFUL, HAPPY PEOPLE ADHERE TO IT.

ANYONE WITH HALF A BRAIN KNOWS THAT.
I KNOW EVERYONE KNOWS THAT! I'M NOT STUPID!

WELL, THIS IS GOODBYE.
ew germs

I'M SORRY, COCO, BUT THIS IS A ONE-WAY TICKET.

HEY! NO FAIR!
I'LL TRY TO FIX WHAT I CAN. I'LL SEND YOU A POSTCARD OR SOMETHING.
clik clik clik

M-MARY?!

WHAT... WHERE DID SHE GO?!

DON'T LOOK AT ME. I WAS DOUBLE-CROSSED TOO.

DIRTY, STUPID STUPID-FACE.

IT... WORKED.

IT WORKED!!!
OH MY GOD, MY OLD **ROOM**--!

MRS. STUFFLES!

MY MORPHIMALS BOOKS!!

I AM SO CUTE!

I LOVE YOU. CAN WE BE FRIENDS?

I'M NOT SCARED OF YOU ANYMORE! YOU HAVE NO POWER OVER ME!
SNAP!

MARY? YOU READY FOR SCHOOL?
Knock knock
I'M--

I'M STILL GETTING DRESSED!
WHAT DAY IS IT TODAY?

YOU KNOW HOW TO FIND OUT WHAT DAY IT IS.
JESUS, MOM, I'M LIKE SEVEN! CAN'T YOU JUST--

LANGUAGE! HOW CAN YOU TALK TO YOUR OWN MOTHER LIKE THAT?
S-SORRY.

YOU'RE GOING TO MISS THE BUS!
I'M JUST IN A... RUSH...

WOW, THE OLD BATHROOM!
HAHAHA!

STOP, STOP! YOU'RE JUST TOO MUCH!
POOF
WHOA, YOU'RE SO BIG.
I GUESS I HAVEN'T LOST ALL THE BABY WEIGHT YET...
mawee!

...WHERE'S THE BUS STOP AGAIN?
HAHA!
GOOD ONE, MARY. WHAT, DO YOU WANT ME TO DROP YOU OFF? THAT WAY YOU CAN SHOW THE BABY FOR SHOW-AND-TELL?
POOF!

ACTUALLY, I RETHOUGHT THAT IDEA. I WOULDN'T WANT HER VANISHING AND RUNNING OFF IN THE SCHOOL, GETTING LOST OR HURT, YOU KNOW...

WHAT A RESPONSIBLE BIG SISTER YOU ARE.
Kiss
NOW RUN ALONG.

35
THIS IS SO WEIRD! HAH!

OH! THERE IT IS!
Turtles!!

OKAY, MARY, TIME TO START ANEW. BE A GOOD PERSON. MAKE GOOD DECISIONS.
UNMAKE YOUR MANY, MANY BAD DECISIONS.
BE A GOOD PERSON.

...TURTLES LIVE LIKE 200 YEARS. OR MORE.
NO WAY!!

TURTLES

AREN'T YOU **RAJ**?

nod
IS THIS SEAT TAKEN?

I STILL CAN'T BELIEVE I WENT TO SCHOOL WITH **THE** RAJ ROY.

YOU'RE, LIKE, REALLY **SPECIAL**. REALLY **AWESOME**.

I THINK YOU THINK I'M SOMEONE ELSE.

YOU SEE **JIMMY** OVER THERE? HE'S **SOOO** CONFIDENT.

TURTLES!!!
Ew turtles are GROSS
FIRE EXIT
HE ENDS UP **MURDERING** HIS **GIRLFRIEND.**
YOU THINK HE'S GOING TO MURDER **JESSICA?!**

SHOULD WE... TELL THE BUS DRIVER?

A DIFFERENT JESSICA. IT'S GOING TO HAPPEN IN, LIKE, TWENTY YEARS. DON'T WORRY.
WHY ARE YOU SAYING THIS STUFF?!

IT'S BECAUSE I'M **PSYCHIC.**

ARE YOU A...

PSYCHICPATH?!

OH MY GOD, KIDS ARE SO DUMB, IT'S ADORABLE!

TOWNSVILLE ELEME

W-WOW, MARY, YOUR CURSIVE IS **AMAZING**!

THANKS, MISS SATKOWSKI!

FGH

HOW DID YOU **DRAW** THIS?! IT'S **INCREDIBLE**!

I JUST DREW WHAT I SAW...

EVERYONE GATHER ROUND AND LOOK AT WHAT **MARY** DID!
Mary Posa 1996

4 HOURS LATER
...THE TWO TIMES TABLE IS TOUGH, BUT I BELIEVE IN YOU KIDS!
Learn Stuff

This is too easy, it's just PAINFUL!

scribble

I know
the three
tims tabls
This is s
easy, i
PAIN

...SO ANYWAY, NEVER GIVE UP ON YOUR DREAMS.

AND YOUR DREAMS SHOULD BE MAKING STUFF FOR COMPUTERS. LIKE... WEBSITES.
turtles

MICROBLOGGING WEBSITES, TO BE SPECIFIC.

THAT SOUNDS REALLY HARD.

IT'S YOUR **DESTINY**, RAJ! YOU'RE THE **CHOSEN ONE!** IF YOU **FAIL**, THE ENTIRE WORLD WILL FALL TO **SHAMBLES!**
THE **OCEANS** WILL RUN **RED** WITH... WITH **WHALE BLOOD!**
HUH?!

ALL THE WHALES WILL DIE IF YOU DON'T ACHIEVE YOUR TRUE POTENTIAL!
?!
THEY'RE ON THE BRINK OF **EXTINCTION**! BUT **YOU** CAN SAVE THEM.

...AND IN REPAYMENT FOR THIS MESSAGE, YOU HAVE TO BE NICE TO ME FOREVER. AND GIVE ME MONEY. OKAY?

MARY LOVES RAJ! EWWWW!
OKAY.
TURN

YOU KNOW, IT'S REALLY FITTING THAT YOU WEAR PIGTAILS, AMANDA.

HUH?

Because you're a LITTLE PIG.

HA
HA
HA
HA
HA

B-BUT... YOU'RE...

YOU'RE WEARING ONE PIGTAIL!
IT'S CALLED A PONYTAIL, AMANDA. AND PONIES ARE AWESOME.

LITTLE PIG
HA
HA
HA
OH MAN, THAT FELT AMAZING. I'VE BEEN WAITING FOR THAT FOR LIKE 20 YEARS.

...YES, I KNOW, SHE'S A CLEVER CHILD.
NO-- THIS IS UNLIKE ANYTHING I'VE EVER SEEN, MRS. POSA. I BELIEVE MARY MIGHT BE...

GIFTED.

WE MADE THESE COOL NECKLACES IN ART CLASS TODAY!
E

HERE YOU GO, PAIGE!
OH, HOW SWEET.

CAN YOU SAY MAR-EE, PAIGEY POO?
MAWEE!
WHO'S SO SMART!

WHAT'S THE SQUARE ROOT OF 122?
SKritch

ELEVEN.

...WHAT'S 343 × 986?

UM...

SORRY, KIDDO. JUST TESTING YOU.

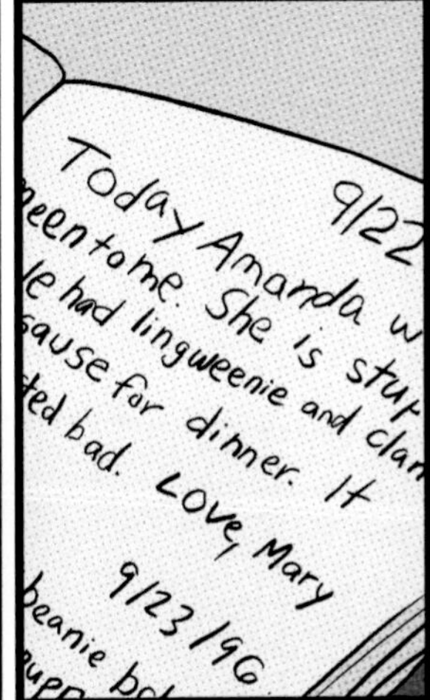
9/22
Today Amanda w
eentome. She is stup
e had lingweenie and clam
sause for dinner. It
ted bad. Love, Mary
9/23/96
beanie bo

ARE YOU PULLING MY LEG?

A Super Family

Chapter 4:
The Return of the Pointed Rogue!

Some villains just don't know when to qui
The Pointed Rogue was one of them. It was
a lovely evening, September 23, and Roman
had only just come home from a long day at
work. I had been on my feet for a long shift at
the nursing home, and wasn't really in the mo
to fight crime. But criminals don't plan around
your schedule. Do you know what the hardest
art of being crime-fighting parents is? Findi
babysitter at the last minute when a vil
cides to hold a reporter hostage—

ckily, I had
es to

TOMORROW, THE **POINTED ROGUE** WILL RETURN...
HE'LL BE... HOLDING A REPORTER HOSTAGE...

HOW DID YOU KNOW?!
ABOUT THE **POINTED ROGUE?!**

9/30/96
MARY POSA
IQ RESULTS:
157*
*has IQ of average 26-year-old
WKAG
ON AIR
AND WE'RE BACK WITH **THE PSYCHIC TOT!** ANY PREDICTIONS FOR THE BIG **GAME** ON SUNDAY?

WELL, I SHOULDN'T ANNOUNCE SPORTS STATS BECAUSE I COULD RUIN THINGS. LIKE IF EVERYONE BETS ON THE WINNING TEAM.
OR IF MY PREDICTION GIVES THE WINNING TEAM A **FALSE** SENSE OF **CONFIDENCE**, CAUSING THEM TO SLACK OFF.

YOU'VE GOT A POINT. BUT YOU'LL TELL ME AFTER THE **SHOW**, RIGHT?

OH, SURE. AND A PREDICTION FOR YOUR FIELD OF WORK: IN THE **FUTURE**, THERE WILL BE... **SATELLITE RADIO.**
I HAVE NO IDEA WHAT THAT MEANS, BUT IT **SOUNDS** COOL!

OH, SWEETHEART.

THIS IS AMAZING. YOU'RE LIKE **ME** AND **DAD** AND LITTLE **PAIGE.**

MY LITTLE GIRL IS **SPECIAL.**

WE'RE SO **PROUD** OF YOU!

YOU SEEM REALLY RELIEVED, MOM.
I **ALWAYS** BELIEVED IN YOU!!!

I'M STILL THE SAME **PERSON**, WITH OR WITHOUT MY **PSYCHIC ABILITY.**

OH, **HONEY**. YOUR POWER IS A **PART** OF YOU. YOU'LL REALIZE THAT WHEN YOU'RE **OLDER.**

DO YOU THINK SHE SHOULD START GOING TO **SUPERHERO AFTERSCHOOL?**
OH GOLLY, WOULD I LOVE THAT!

THE
RODNEY CUMMERBUND
AFTERSCHOOL FOR
GIFTED YOUNG'UNS.
Fostering tomorrow's
bright future

FWOOSH

heh heh
AHHH!!
LITTLE GOOD BOY, YOU PUT HIM DOWN THIS INSTANT!
COUNSELOR
WHAT ARE YOU GONNA DO, TELL MY PARENTS?
COME ON, THAT'S NOT FAIR...
BECAUSE THEY'RE DEAD, FROOZIE. I DON'T THINK THEY'RE GOING TO PUNISH ME.
MY PARENTS...
FWOOOO
ARE DEAD!!!

OKAY...
NOW TRY THE NEXT ONE.
...

WAHHH
"ABNORMAL STRENGTH." WELL, MAYBE THAT'LL DEVELOP WITH TIME.
HNGH...
KREEE

I FORESEE ...
SLAM!

GREAT PAIN... AND DEATH AT AN EARLY AGE...

...DID I SAY "ABNORMAL STRENGTH"?! I MEANT... VERY IMPRESSIVE, WOW, WAY TO GO, KIDDO.
OKAY, NOW, RUN ALONG TO THE "DEAD PARENTS: PRODUCTIVELY CHANNELING YOUR PAIN" SEMINAR!

UGH, PSYCHO TOT. WHERE DO THEY FIND THESE KIDS?!
SKIP

IT'S SO INSPIRING TO SEE SUCH TALENTED YOUNGSTERS!
YOU'VE GOT YOUR **WHOLE** LIFE AHEAD OF YOU, LITTLE LADY--
WHAT DO YOU WANT TO DO WITH IT?
SAVE THE WORLD. BE A GOOD PERSON. THAT KIND OF STUFF.
OH, YOU'RE **ALREADY** A GOOD PERSON! AND JUST SO **ADORABLE!**
HOW DOES IT FEEL TO BE SO CUTE, **AND** SMARTER THAN ALL THE ADULTS?
IT...
MARY
OH MY **GOD,** NOT NOW, NO NO NO--
FEELS... KIND OF HOLLOW...
?
AW, UH, CHEER UP, KID!
MAR
CAN YOU HEAR

MARY? HONEY?
MARY
BLEEP
UM
WUH--WHERE DID YOU LEARN THAT LAN--
OKAY, PINE ELEVEN. THE GLORBON INVASION. FROOZIE WILL DIE DURING THAT.
THE ECONOMY WILL TANK IN '08. SO, FUTURE COLLEGE ATTENDEES: CHOOSE THE CHEAPER SCHOOL.
THE, THE INDIGENOUS PEOPLES WILL WIN THE SUPER GOAL THIS YEAR.
S-SWEETIE-
I--I SWEAR I'M NOT LYI--

--NG.
MARY?
YOU'RE ALIVE.
YOU--
YOU BROKE THE **TIMEKEEPER**?!
YEP.
YOU'VE RUINED **EVERYTHING!** BUT...
SHAKE
Sorry...
WHY AREN'T THINGS **DIFFERENT?**
SLUMP
PROBABLY BECAUSE YOU WERE GONE FOR LIKE **THIRTY SECONDS?**

DAILY PLAN
PSYCHIC TOT A FRAU
FLAME GIRL & EL ROMANCERO: "WE MESSED UP"
WHY AM I HERE...?
OH MY GOD... I MADE IT SO MUCH WORSE.
FOR SALE
ha ha
What's a time crystal?
URL: http://conspiracynerds.com
CONSPIRACY NERDS
if only you knew what we know...
Thread: Remember Psychic Tot?
outsidejob22 1/24/1998
We believe you, Psychic Tot!
r0sw311 1/25/1998
I wonder what she meant by Glorbon Invasion? Could it have already happened?!
bohemiancrapsody 1/25/1998
are YOU a glorbon?
GET your GLORB on!
GLORB
you put a TIME CRYSTAL on your LITTLE SISTER? what is WRONG with you?
Jesus Christ. Don't pretend you don't know.

MARY... WERE YOU THAT **PSYCHIC TOT?**

HOW... DID I NOT... RECOGNIZE...?
COCO... I NEED THE BLANKET.

I THOUGHT YOU WERE GOING TO FIX MY LIFE, TOO! **HM?!**

I GAVE YOU STOCK TIPS. **CHRIST.** YOU SHOULD BE GLAD I DIDN'T SCREW YOUR LIFE UP **MORE.**

THAT... THAT WAS ***YOU?***

BUT... MY GREAT **WEALTH** WAS AN INTRINSIC PART OF MY **TRAGIC PAST.**

THIS **BLANKET** ISN'T HELPING AT ALL.

?
FWOOSH

HOW CAN I SHOW MY FACE IN PUBLIC AGAIN?

HENCHGIRL
KRISTEN GUDSNUK

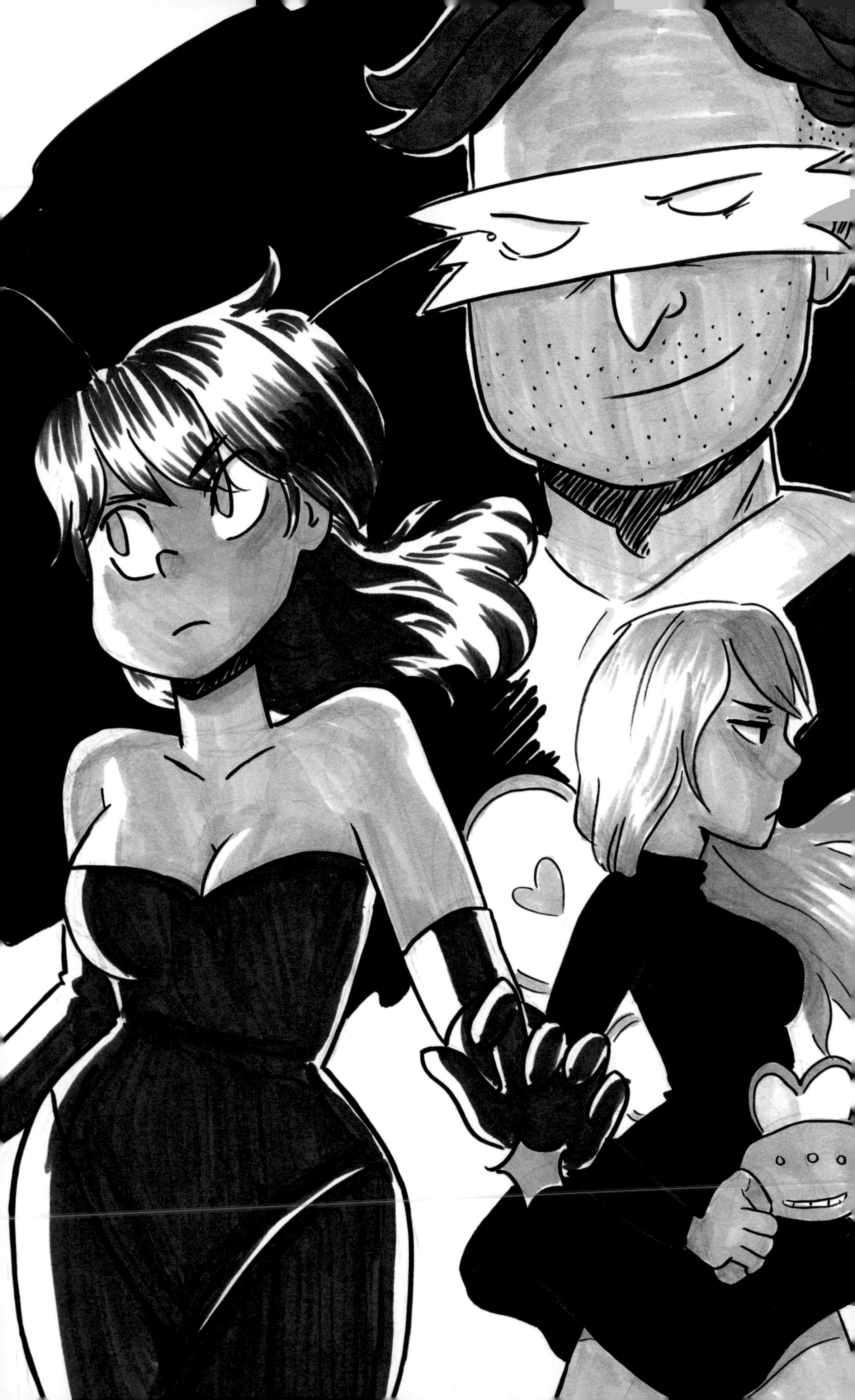

¡¡DETENTE,
MALVADA!!
CONSUELO?
HOW DO YOU-- I MEAN... TH-THAT'S NOT MY NAME!
YO SOY LA VIUDA!
VILLAINS! DON'T YOU REMEMBER ...
CRAZY SWORD LADY. AND THIS IS WHERE WE LEAVE.
SAVE YOURSELF.
LEAVE ME TO MY MISERY.
THWOMP

WEREN'T YOU A... MAID-THEMED HERO?
...WAS I? ESO ME PARECE UN POCO **ESTEREOTÍPICO...**
WIPE

PERO... **FAMILIAR.**
GOD, YOU'RE HEAVY.
SHUT UP!

¡MALVADAS! YOU RUINED MY **LIFE!**
Let me out

MY LAST-DITCH EXIT STRATEGY.

...THE **GRAPPLING HOOK.**
I DON'T KNOW HOW TO USE THAT THING!

PREPÁRATE A MORIR.

WHAT DO I CARE.
FWOMP
WHY DID I TAKE **FRENCH** IN HIGH SCHOOL?!

WHO ARE--
POOF

POOF!
huff huff
YOU'RE HEAVY.
?!
UM...
YOU'RE WELCOME?
...
WHO ARE YOU?
IT'S SECRET.
HENCE...
WHY DO YOU KEEP...
...SAVING ME?
POOF
...

STOMP STOMP

OH, THERE YOU ARE. THANKS FOR ALL THE HELP.

WHAT HAPPENED, ANYWAY?
WHATEVER HAPPENED... THAT'S HOW I GOT AWAY FROM THE COPS THAT TIME.

LUCKY. I DON'T HAVE SOME MYSTERY PERSON WHISKING ME AWAY WHENEVER I'M IN TROUBLE.

SO WE RUINED CONSUELO'S LIFE?

GOD, IT RINGS A BELL BUT HONESTLY, MY HEAD IS KINDA JUMBLED.

WHAT AM I GONNA DO?!
YOU SHOULD JUST TRY TO STAY OUT OF TROUBLE, IF THAT'S EVEN REMOTELY POSSIBLE.

GO TO MY APARTMENT.
NO MORE SCHEMES FOR A BIT, OKAY?
BUT I HAVEN'T EVEN GOTTEN REVENGE ON AMELIA YET. OR MONSIEUR B.
FWSH!

MAYBE I CAN COUP D'ÉTAT **THE BUTTERFLY GANG.**
COOL IT WITH THE SCHEMES! WHAT DID MONSIEUR B EVER DO TO **YOU?**
AS IF YOU HAVE TO **ASK!**
...
...AREN'T YOU COMING WITH?
I HAVE SOMETHING TO DO.
SOMETHING I SHOULD HAVE DONE...
...LONG AGO...
'KAY, BYE.
SIGH
GET OUT.
NO WAY. I COME BEARING **INTEL.**

THE BUTTERFLY DEN
HELLOOOO?
HEY, LARRY, IS MONSIEUR B AROUND?
NAW...
TELL HIM-- LARRY?
CRASH

SPRAY IT PAINT SO!
Threatening Red TM

YOU'RE NEXT
PFFFFF
TELL MONSIEUR B I SAID...

TELL HIM I DID THIS.
LARRY?

sigh
PFF

YOU'RE NEXT
- MARY

AND THAT'S BASICALLY MY TRAGIC BACKSTORY.

THAT WAS VERY... **SAD**, COCO. AND, UH, YOUR SAT SCORE REALLY **WAS** IMPRESSIVE.
WAS... WAS **THAT** WHAT YOU CAME HERE TO TELL ME?

THERE'S SOMETHING I LEFT OUT.

SOMETHING I ... DIDN'T PUT TOGETHER... UNTIL IT HAPPENED TO MARY.
MONSIEUR BUTTERFLY GOT HIS PAL **DR. MANIAC** TO INJECT MARY WITH SOMETHING CALLED **EVIL SERUM.**
IT REQUIRED A CHEMICAL CALLED **L-47.**

"EVIL SERUM"?
THAT'S WHAT YOU STOLE FROM MY LAB. YES... I SUPPOSE IT COULD INTERFERE WITH FRONTAL LOBE RECEPTORS...

BUT IT WOULDN'T BE SO TERRIBLY **DRASTIC**. I CERTAINLY WOULDN'T EXPECT ATTEMPTED **HOMICIDE** FROM THIS SOLUTION. LACK OF EMPATHY, MAYBE A FEW OUTSTANDING **PARKING TICKETS** OR SOMETHING.
I HAVE OUTSTANDING PARKING TICKETS...
Scribble

TINA, TRUST ME, YOU HAVE NOT BEEN **EVIL SERUM'D.**

I GOT THIS WEIRD DÉJÀ VU WHEN I WAS THERE. I FELT LIKE... IT HAD HAPPENED TO ME, TOO.
BUT IF YOU'RE **EVIL,** WHY DO YOU CARE?

HOW WOULD **YOU** FEEL IF SOMETHING ELSE WAS CONTROLLING YOUR DECISIONS?

ALL THIS TIME I THOUGHT I WAS DOING THIS FOR ME...
THAT SUCKS.
YEAH, I GUESS THE LIFE OF CRIME ISN'T COOL AFTER ALL. YOU DODGED A BULLET THERE, KID.
COCOA

WELL, I'M GOING TO NEED TO SEE THE ENTIRE MAKEUP OF THE SERUM TO DEVISE THE ANTIDOTE.

YOU THINK YOU CAN **DO** THAT?
COCOA

CHEMISTRY IS **MY** SUPERPOWER.

BY WHICH I MEAN, ***THEORETICALLY*** I SHOULD BE ABLE TO MAKE AN ANTIDOTE.

DON'T QUOTE ME ON THAT OR ANYTHING.
BUT I'D NEED A SAMPLE OF THE SERUM.

WE CAN INVADE THE OFFICE AT NIGHT! I CAN MAKE A CARROT ARMY!

YOU COULD GET KILLED! NO WAY!!
Krsh!

IT'S THE ONLY WAY.
Tina...

MAYBE WE CAN GET FRED TO HELP. OR EVEN PHOTO-GIRL.

YOU **BETTER** NOT HAVE BEEN READING MY ONLINE JOURNAL.

HAH! YOU WISH.

TELL ME THAT'S NOT ANOTHER EVIL PLAN.
IT'S THERAPEUTIC.
EVIL PLAN 2.0
This time, it's personal
YIP YIP

LOOK, MARY, YOU JUST HAVE TO SIT TIGHT FOR A FEW DAYS.
I ACTUALLY HAVE A PLAN THAT COULD ***FIX***...
BEEP!

DID YOU BREAK INTO THE BUTTERFLY DEN AND... BREAK THE ***PROJECTOR?***

MAYBE.

OH MY GOD! I WAS GONE FOR LIKE AN ***HOUR.***

I SAID IT'S ***THERAPEUTIC.***

THAT PROJECTOR WAS HD AND COST LIKE FIVE HUNDRED BUCKS. MONSIEUR B TOLD ME TO TELL YOU YOU'RE FIRED.
WASN'T I FIRED ALREADY?

THIS IS WHAT HAPPENS WHEN YOU MESS WITH THE TIMELINE!

PLSHH

HAVE SOME TEA, IDIOT.
WITTY SLOGA

no, you.

TEA
EEPYTIME
contains. tea, chamomille, valium
EEPYTIME®
Rx
Sleeping pills

I'M NOT GONNA LET YOU RUIN THIS FOR ME.
Z Z Z Z Z Z Z

TREES
EUGENE MANIAC, MD
"Nothing to See Here!"

CLOSED

I DON'T KNOW WHY I SHOULD BE HELPING MARY.
CONSUELO–

TIME BARON! CALL ME LA VIUDA!

THE CAT'S ALREADY OUT OF THE BAG, CONSUELO. WE KNOW YOU'RE NAMED CONSUELO.
ANYWAY, THIS IS FOR THE GREATER GOOD.
viuda.

THIS GUY HAS BEEN TURNING HENCHPEOPLE EVIL. THERE COULD BE MANY MORE.
IF WE MAKE AN ANTIDOTE, WE COULD REDUCE CRIME MORE EXPEDIENTLY THAN...

...THAN BY SIMPLY BEATING BAD GUYS INTO SUBMISSION. I SWEAR, I WILL NEVER GET USED TO THAT.
sorry
SQULCH
Relay Science '09

I GUESS I'LL SCOPE THE PLACE OUT NOW.

PLEASE, TAKE CARE OF MY BODY.

FWOOo

KRRR

AHHHHH
SCIENCE!
09

GLUE
KRK
glue

IT'S **STUCK** TO MY **HAND**!

WELL, THAT'S WHY WE BROUGHT **THIS** STUFF.
PAPIER MÂCHÉ

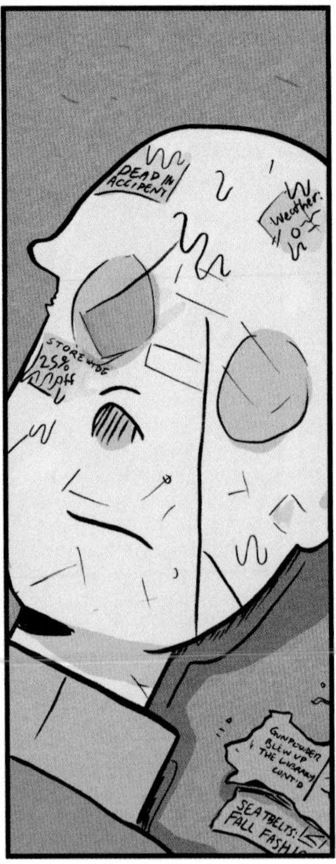
DEAD IN ACCIDENT
Weather
STOREWIDE 25% off
GUNPOWDER BLEW UP THE LIBRARY CONT'D
SEATBELTS: FALL FASHI

25
UM, BAD NEWS.

THERE ARE... **FOUR** GUARDS INSIDE.
skrtch skrtch
WHO COULD **POSSIBLY** WANT THAT MANY **GUARDS?!!!**
evil serum/ file cabinet
chemical shelf
don't go in here (trust me)
hall
bathroom
closet
X = guard
room
hall
desk
tv
couch
IT REALLY SEEMS EXCESSIVE.
DON'T WORRY! MY **CARROT ARMY** CAN TAKE THEM ON.
...AND **MI ESPADA** CAN HANDLE LOS DEMAS!
CARLOT, YOUR TASK IS TO PROTECT SUE AT ALL COSTS.
UM... MORE BAD NEWS.
Beep!

MARY GOT AWAY. SHE'S GOING AFTER **AMELIA** AGAIN.
!

FRED, YOU SHOULD GO HELP MARY. SHE MIGHT... LISTEN TO YOU.

...
WE CAN HANDLE THESE GUARDS. SERÁ BASTANTE FÁCIL.

GOOD LUCK...

FREE PAMPHLETS
ask about
ASSISTED
SUICIDE
¡Venganza!
POW!
RADD
Steve
CHNG
What the HECK
GUY
THIS WAY!

huff huff
TINA! LOOK OUT!
BLOCK!!
JUST-- GET THE-- THING!!
FILE
HYA!
heh
LURCH
AHHH!
ACID
CLANGG

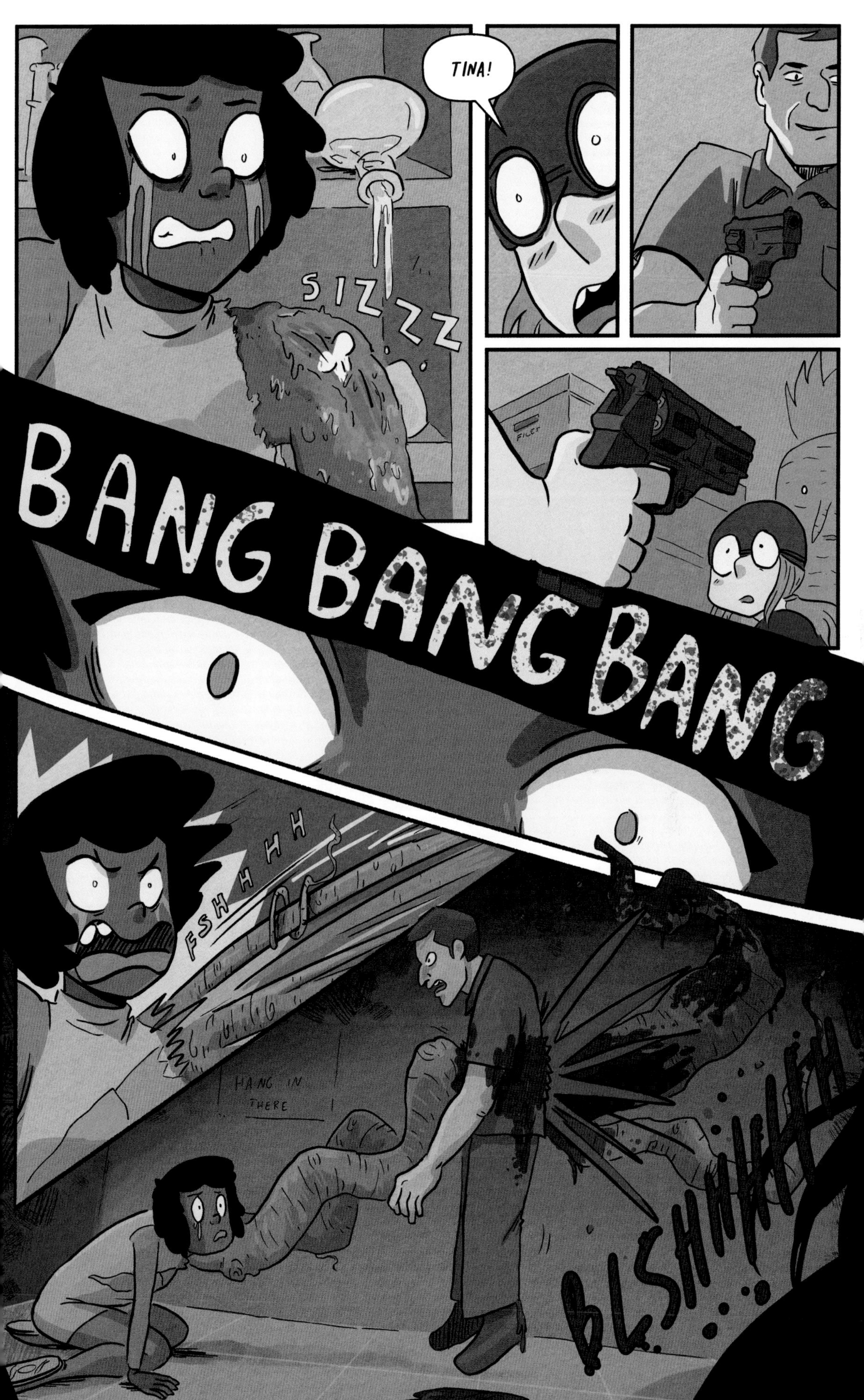
SIZZZ
TINA!
FILES
BANG BANG BANG BANG
FSHHHHH
HANG IN THERE
BLSHHHHH

TINA?!
DID YOU GET THE SERUM?
MORE ACID

Y-YEAH. ARE YOU OKAY?
nghh...

SLITHHHH

I... THINK SO.
SLITHHH

YOU DID A GOOD JOB, CARLOT.

RUN!
¿QUÉ DIABLOS OCURRIÓ? THESE CRIATURAS ARE ATACÁNDOME!

TINA! WAKE UP!
CREPE CITY

SI ESTAS ZANAHORIAS MALVADAS HACEN DAÑO A MI COCHE...

HUH? THAT'S... THAT'S NOT SUPPOSED TO HAPPEN.

THUDD

UM... I KILLED A GUY BACK THERE.

YOU **SAVED** ME.

...I USED TO BE **AFRAID** OF KILLING PEOPLE.

BUT AFTER I KILLED GUNPOWDER--
YOU KILLED GUNPOWDER?
WHAT, DO YOU LIVE UNDER A ROCK OR SOMETHING?

...ANYWAY, NOW I REALIZE IT'S JUST EXPEDITING THE INEVITABLE.
AND REALLY, I'M ACTUALLY HELPING THE EARTH BY REMOVING YOUR CARBON FOOTPRINT--
I'M A VEGAN! MY CARBON FOOTPRINT IS NEGLIGIBLE!

YEAH, WELL, OVERPOPULATION IS GOING TO BECOME A BIG PROBLEM IN THE NEXT 50 YEARS OR SO, ACCORDING TO THIS DOCUMENTARY I WATCHED.
TURTLE RECALL

AND YOU SEEM LIKE THE TYPE TO PROCREATE.
W-WHO KNOWS? I MIGHT BE BARREN!

STOP!!
IS THAT MY SHIRT?

FRED! AND... COCO? YOU GUYS DOING A TEAM-UP OR SOMETHING?
TURTLE RECALL

MARY. YOU HAVE TO STOP THIS.
I ACTUALLY AGREE. JUST COME WITH US; WE CAN FIX YOU.

HA! YOU CAN'T FIX ANYTHING. I'VE RUINED EVERYTHING IRREPARABLY.
MAY AS WELL TAKE DOWN THIS...

...THIS HOMEWRECKER WHILE I'M AT IT.
HOMEWRECKER?! WHOSE HOME HAVE I WRECKED?
TURTLE RECALL

YOU'VE RUINED MY LIFE! YOU STOLE MY...

...BOYFRIEND...

WHO, FRED? ARE YOU TWO AN ITEM?!

I DON'T SEE THE NEED TO PUT LABELS ON EVERYTHING.
UGH! MEN.
PUSH

BUT WHAT HAVE I DONE? I DON'T UNDERSTAND.
FRED AND I ARE JUST FRIENDS.
MAYBE YOU CAN ASK YOUR GOD WHEN YOU DIE.

SHE'S NOT THE ONE WHO RUINED YOUR LIFE. THINK ABOUT IT LOGICALLY.
Pat!

YOU RUINED YOUR OWN LIFE.

SO YOU'RE ON HER SIDE?!

YOUR LIFE ISN'T OVER YET. SERIOUSLY, JUST COME WITH US.
YOU'VE BEEN DRUGGED. YOU'RE NOT ENTIRELY IN CONTROL OF YOUR ACTIONS.
HAH! A LIKELY STORY.
WE CAN HELP YOU--
MAYBE IF YOU HELPED ME WHEN I ACTUALLY ASKED FOR YOUR HELP, FRED.

IT'S TOO LATE.

THE **ANGELIC SCEPTER!** YOUR MOST POWERFUL ARTIFACT! WE'VE *FOUND* IT AT LAST!

NO, YOU DUMB CAT, THIS IS CALLED THE **MONARCH SCEPTER.**
TURTLE RECALL

BUTTERFLY--
C'MON, MARY, CUT IT OUT.
Sigh...

HEY!
FWOOO
TURTLE RECALL

POOF

OKAY, I DID **NOT** SIGN UP FOR THIS.

MARY!

WHAT--WHAT'S GOING **ON**?

POOF

...

TURTLE RECALL

Amelia?

?

FZZSHHHH

COCO?
TURTLE RECALL

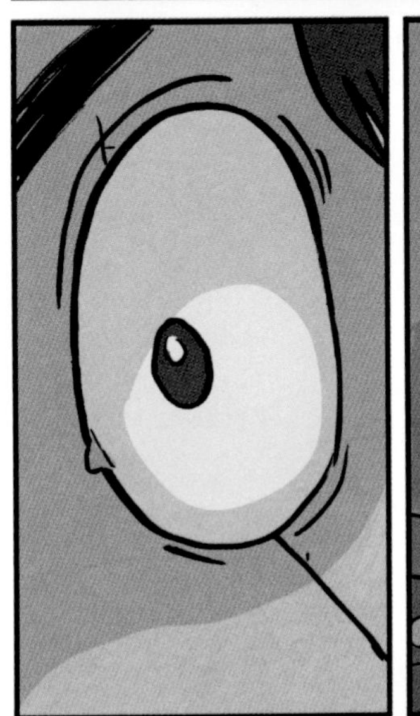

COME ON, S-STUPID BLANKET...

COCO?!

CRUMPLE

YOU HAVE BEEN JUDGED...

WORTHY.

C'MON, MARY, WE'VE GOTTA GET OUT OF HERE--
YOU HAVE BEEN JUDGED...
C-COCO?
TURTLE RECALL

WORTHY.

AND YOU HAVE BEEN JUDGED...
TURTLE RECALL

LEAST WORTHY OF ALL.
MARY! LOOK OUT!
CRUMBLE
SHOVE
FZZ
SHH

RUMBLE
MARY?! OH, GOD--
CRASHH

P-Paige?

YOU'RE ALIVE!

KRRR-
FZZZZ?
SAY CHEESE!
UNWORTHY.
RUN!
YANK!
FRED--

RRRRRR
huff huff

W-WE HAVE TO SAVE FRED...

POOF

FLOOP

Schedule

SHE'S AWAKE!
Schedule: Dr. Mario
HOW MUCH DOES IT HURT?
Medications:
Allergies: Hard work lol

PLEASE TELL ME THAT WAS ALL A DREAM.
A REALLY LONG, VIVID DREAM.
Schedule: Dr. Mario

ON THE PLUS SIDE, YOU'RE YOU AGAIN.

YOU GOT DOSED WITH EVIL SERUM AND SUE GAVE YOU AN ANTIDOTE.
I MEAN, THAT WASN'T REALLY YOU DOING ALL THAT STUFF.

YEAH, IT WAS.

WELL, DON'T SAY THAT IN COURT.

SPEAKING OF WHICH, I'M SOMEWHAT CONFIDENT THAT YOU CAN GET THE CHARGES **DROPPED**.
I'D FEEL **BETTER** IF YOU COULD GET A GREAT LAWYER, BUT THEY'VE **FROZEN** YOUR **ASSETS**--
YOUR **SURPRISINGLY AMPLE** ASSETS--
I HAD **NO CLUE** YOU WERE SO **RICH!**
...DO YOU EVEN **KNOW** WHAT YOUR **STOCK PORTFOLIO** IS VALUED AT?

I GUESS I... FORGOT ABOUT THOSE? IT'S COMPLICATED.

ANYWAY, YOU WEREN'T ACTING OF YOUR OWN VOLITION.
AT LEAST, SOME OF THE TIME.

YEAH, BUT... I **KILLED** GUNPOWDER.

GUNPOWDER BLEW UP A **LIBRARY** THIS MORNING, SO I'M PRETTY SURE HE'S STILL KICKING AROUND. HE WAS REALLY MAD THAT HIS FAVORITE CHARACTER DIED IN **DRAGONFINDER: ACT OF THE APOLLONIANS.**
...AFTER THEY **FINALLY** FINISHED RENOVATIONS FROM THE GLORBON INVASION...

OH. I GUESS I... **DIDN'T** KILL GUNPOWDER. SO WHY AM I CUFFED TO THE BED, EXACTLY?
YOU STILL DID SOME NASTY STUFF, MARY. **ARMED ROBBERY, TRESPASSING, HOOLIGANISM, ATTEMPTED MURDER**--
AND THE **L-47** SERUM YOU WERE DOSED WITH...

IT WASN'T ACTUALLY IN YOUR SYSTEM BY THE TIME THE HOSPITAL LET ME DO A BLOOD TEST. BUT THAT DOESN'T MEAN IT WASN'T STILL AFFECTING YOU, RIGHT?
SCIENCE'S APPLICATION IN HUMAN PSYCHOLOGY IS STILL VERY INCOMPLETE.

I MOCKED UP A FAKE BLOOD PANEL.
IT SHOULD HOLD UP IN COURT.
YOU COULD GET IN **TROUBLE.**

MY FAKE BLOOD PANEL IS VERY CONVINCING.
shrug
MARY?

HI.
SCUZZ

MOM AND DAD WERE HERE BEFORE. THERE'S A **GALACTIC DISRUPTION** AND THEY HAD TO, YOU KNOW...
SAVE THE UNIVERSE AGAIN.
shedool

LIKE, **C'MON,** PRIORITIES, GUYS.

IT'S A PRETTY GOOD EXCUSE.
heh

WHEN THE CEILING COLLAPSED ON YOU, I WAS **SURE** YOU'D... YOU'D...

DIED?
UM... YEAH.

IT'S, LIKE, A MEDICAL MIRACLE YOU'RE ALIVE.

MISS POSA, THERE'S A NICE YOUNG MAN HERE TO SEE YOU.

F-FRED?

NEWS
Schedule: Dr Mario
To Do:
① make to-do list
② ?
...

MARY! I'VE FINALLY FOUND YOU!
SLAM!

UM, WHO ARE YOU?

RAJ ROY, FOUNDER OF MUMBLR.

I LEFT MY FIANCÉE. AND NOW, MY BEAUTIFUL MARY, I'LL FIX EVERYTHING FOR YOU.
"fiancée"?

I'VE GOTTEN YOU THE BEST LAWYERS. I'VE PAID YOUR BAIL.

BUT... WHAT HAPPENED, EXACTLY?

THAT CRAZY GIRL DESTROYED A BUILDING IN THE **ABANDONED WAREHOUSE DISTRICT.** YOUR SISTER TRIED TO SAVE EVERYONE...
I COULDN'T SAVE EVERYONE.

Okay, when did THAT happen?
Tina powered up.
SQUIFFFFF

VOLUME
ALIEN CAT

YOU CAN'T DO THIS! THE CATACLYSM IS COMING!!
COP

YOU'LL NEED MY HELP!!
YEAH, YEAH, TELL THAT TO GEORGE PAUL FRANCIS.
COP

LOOK AT THAT. VAGUE CATACLYSMIC PREDICTIONS. NOT LIKE YOU. YOU GAVE DATES AND DETAILS.
I ALWAYS BELIEVED IN YOUR PSYCHIC POWERS, MARY.
I'M NOT PSYCHIC. I JUST... TIME TRAVELED.

WELL, THAT IS ALSO PRETTY COOL...?

I...
I SAVED JESSICA.

WHO?
DON'T YOU REMEMBER? YOU TOLD ME JIMMY WOULD MURDER A WOMAN NAMED JESSICA IN 20 YEARS' TIME.
OH YEAH.

I FOLLOWED HIM AROUND FOR ALMOST A YEAR. AND I STOPPED HIM.
SHE'D BE DEAD IF IT WEREN'T FOR YOU.

I WAS EVEN GOING TO MARRY HER UNTIL... I SAW YOUR FACE ON THE NEWS.
...I HAD ALMOST CONVINCED MYSELF YOU WERE A FIGMENT OF MY IMAGINATION BY THAT POINT.

I-IS THERE ANY CHANCE YOU CAN... PATCH THINGS UP WITH HER?

JESSICA COMPLETELY UNDERSTANDS.

GEORGE PAUL FRANCIS, STAR OF THE PAJAMA CATS SERIES, WAS ONE OF A DOZEN HOBOES WHO WERE KILLED IN THE COLLAPSE.
TRAGIC DEATH

HE WAS RESEARCHING AN UPCOMING ROLE AS A HOMELESS ASSASSIN...
WHAT ABOUT COCO?
THOUSANDS OF MOURNERS...

SHE... DIDN'T MAKE IT.

AND... FRED?

THEY FOUND SOME CERAMIC PIECES IN THE WRECKAGE. AND THE SHROUD, TORN TO BITS.
I... I THINK... HE'S OUT THERE. SOMEWHERE.

SQUIFFF
WE CAN PUT HIM BACK TOGETHER AGAIN.

SOMEHOW.

I THINK... I NEED TO BE ALONE.

YOU'RE **ALIVE.**
AND AS LONG AS YOU'RE ALIVE, YOU CAN TRY TO SET THINGS **RIGHT.**

CLICK

AND I'M VERY, **VERY** GLAD YOU'RE ALIVE.

10 PM
ONE YEAR LATER
PAWN SHOP / EXPOSITION TOOL
PAWN

PAWN
SKULK
OFFICIAL NOTICE:

10:03

CRAP!
YOU THERE! IT'S PAST CARROTFEW!

I'M RUNNING LATE! I LIVE RIGHT NEARBY!

YOU'LL HAVE TO COME WITH ME, HUMAN.

N-NO...!
SCUZZ

KLANG!

FFEEOOM!!
RUN!
WHAT WAS THAT?!

YOU THERE!
YOU'RE UNDER ARREST FOR ASSAULTING A BETA--
FRED? A LITTLE HELP?

FWOOOO

WIPE
FRED?

H-H-I...
WAVE

KISS

OH, FRED!
RUN... I CAN'T... CONTROL ...

MUCH LON--
THANKS!
VOOM!

I DON'T LIKE CARROT ANYMO
FWIP!

phew!

MARY! WHAT'S YOUR STATUS? COME IN?

PAL AND I RETRIEVED THE MESSENGER. WE GOT HELD UP BY THE **BETA CARROT TEAM**. HE...
PUSH!
KRRR

SHOULD BE FINE. GODDAMN HIM. HE **LET** HIMSELF GET CAUGHT.

"FOR RECON PURPOSES." I'M...
NO TRESPASSIN'
DO NOT PUSH
Beep Boop

I'M BACK.
PLAN:
1.
INTERNET
MARTIAL LAW
sexy lonely carrots

THE **MESSENGER.** I CAN'T BELIEVE IT.

TESTING TESTING TESTING

MY TURN!
YOINK

SEND

BEEP BOOP
IS THIS THING ON?

THE CELESTIAL MESSENGER IS NOT A ***TOY!***
WHAT SHOULD I WRITE, THEN?
HOW ABOUT "BEWARE THE CATACLYSM"?
TRY SOMETHING MORE SPECIFIC. LIKE, "TINA'S CARROTS WILL TAKE OVER CREPE CITY AND...
"MARY TURNED BAD, HELP HER BEFORE SHE GETS YOU KILLED."

IT'S GIVING ME AN ERROR.
SUCH IS THE WAY OF THE **TIMEKEEPER.** IT CAN ONLY RECEIVE NEBULOUS WARNINGS.

WHAT'S THE POINT OF THE DAMN THING?!
sensible cardigans
YOU SWEATER BELIEVE IT!
carrot sighting

MAYBE WE CAN... CHANGE THE PAST.
IF ONLY FRED HADN'T BROKEN THE TIMEKEEPER...

FRED SAYS, "WHY DON'T YOU SEND ME *FIFTY* MESSAGES THAT SAY, 'DON'T BREAK THE TIMEKEEPER.' IT WORKED SO WELL LAST TIME."
FRED:
WHY DON'T
FIFTY MES
TIME KEE
IT WORKE
TIME

HOW ABOUT: "KEEP THE TIMEKEEPER AWAY FROM MARY."
OOH, OR "DON'T EVER LET MARY SEE THE TIMEKEEPER."
"TELL AMELIA NOT TO BLOG ABOUT HER MAGICAL ARTIFACTS."

THAT COULD WORK.

MAYBE...
WE CAN GET COCO BACK.

YEAH.

AND I CAN FINALLY STOP BEING THE FREAKIN' **PSYCHIC TOT.**

BUT YOU WERE SO **CUTE.**

PLAN:
1.
INVASION OF THE BETA CARROT TEAM
MARTIAL LAW IN CREPE CITY
PRESIDENT: "I give up"
VP: "That place sucks anyway"
THERE'S SOMETHING ELSE. PAL THINKS HE FOUND... A **LEAD** ON TINA.

HM. I HADN'T EVEN CONSIDERED...
FRED, SCOPE IT OUT. LET ME KNOW IF YOU CAN FIND ANY SIGN OF HER.

AMELIA, RALLY THE TROOPS.
WE'RE COMING, **TINA.**

YEAH. WE CAN TOTALLY FIX THIS.
RIP

HENCH GAGS

ha ha ha ha

The Amazing Adventures of Coco Oon

NOT WITHOUT YOUR RIDE!

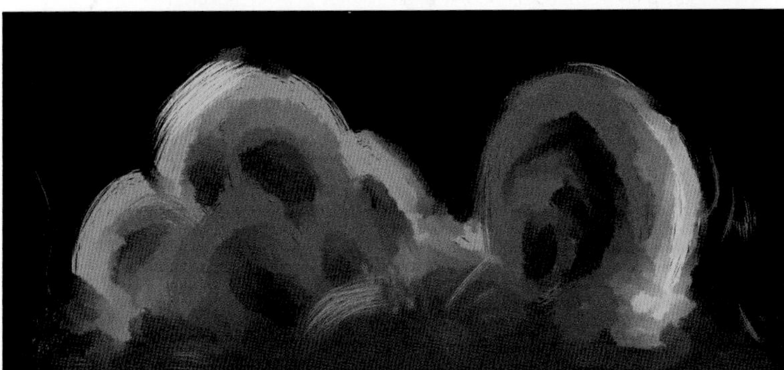

See pages 8–10 and page 25.

HEY FOLKS! IT'S TIME FOR SOME

HENCHGAGS!

PARENTAL GUIDANCE ADVISED

WE ALWAYS HAD HIGH HOPES FOR YOU.

WE ALWAYS KNEW *YOU*, OUR PRECIOUS CHILD, WOULD BRING HONOR TO THE FAMILY NAME.
AWW, THANKS, iDAD.

WHERE DID WE GO WRONG?

BURIED TREASURE

WHAT A LONG DAY...

ERNGH, SOMETHING IS POKING MY BOOB...

YESSSS

Reference pages 37–42.

THE ADVENTURES OF LA MUCAMA!

The Adventures of SUE!

This makes more sense if you've read pages 77 and 93.

THE ADVENTURES OF MR. GREAT GUY!

Fear me, villains!

The Adventures of FRED!

Check out pages 74–75 and 89.

This happened during pages 114–115!

HENCHGAGS

so true lol

HENCHIES

She really liked those goggles

SEÑOR MAL HOMBRE

TOO MANY LOLLIPOPS

Behind the scenes of pages 129 and 133.

THE ADVENTURES of Recuperating Consuelo!

The unforeseen consequences of page 144.

THE ADVENTURES OF CELESTIAL ANGEL AMELIA & THE TIME BARON

HE'S GETTING AWAY! TIME TO TRANSFORM, FRED!
...
POOP CLOSET

The high jinks ensue after the events on pages 176–178.

HENCHGAGS

CON Consuelo

Where Consuelo went during pages 199–205.

DOLLS DOLLS DOLLS!

HENCHDOG!

After Mary left on pages 189–191 and following the origins of Henchdog on page 193.

THE WORST-LAID PLANS...

CREPE BOOK

MESSAGES

You should check out pages 191–193 and page 205 if you don't get these.

HENCHGAGS

Rhonda Pillar

MY BODY GROWS STRONGER--
AS DOES MY WILL TO OVERCOME.

I KNOW MY FAMILY IS DOING THEIR BEST TO FIND ME. IF ONLY THEY KNEW I AM CAPTIVE TO THE **GLORBONS**, FAR FROM THAT BLUE MARBLE, **PLANET EARTH.**
SQUINT

NO MATTER. I MUST HOLD ON TO HOPE.

"Whatever happened to Mary's backpack?"

I'VE FINALLY DISCOVERED MY NEMESES' SECRET IDENTITIES--**AND** THEIR ABODE! AND NOW, ***THE POINTED ROGUE*** WILL WREAK HAVOC!

HOLD THE PHONE-- WHAT'S THIS?!

HEH HEH HEH... THEIR PRECIOUS **SECRETS...**
A SUPER FAMILY

"GERALD CROWLEY, THE **FIRST** POINTED ROGUE, DIED OF... **HEART FAILURE...**
"AT AGE 45. HE WAS DISCOVERED WEEKS LATER IN HIS FILTHY APARTMENT."

Katie Pillar's cousin from page 217.
Mary's time travel adventure and her "psychic tools" arrived on page 224, but only she left on page 240.

HENCHGAGS:

THE FORTUNES OF FROOZIE

Froozie's fate was revealed on page 239.

one last

HENCHGAG

for the road...

The future on pages 283–288.

“IN HIDING”

ISSU
3

GIRL

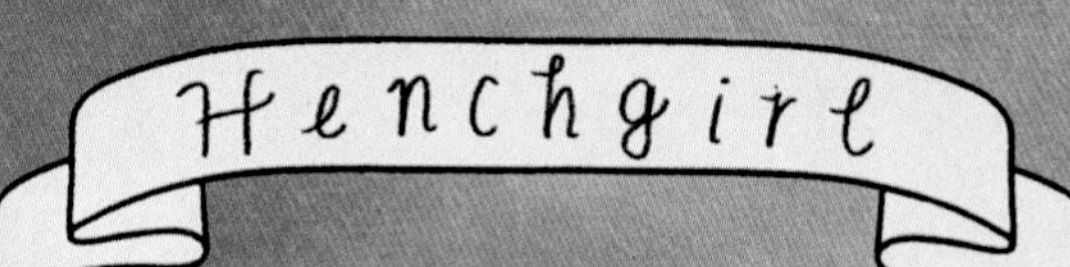

Attitude Adjustment

Love Has No Cure!

Kristen Gudsnuk

EVIL
HENCHGIRL
KRISTEN
GUDSNUK
ISSUE
7
KG

SAY CHEESE!
NIKUMO PHOTOGIRL!
CTHULU

Illustration by
Amanda Cepeda

Illustration by Alexandra Graudins

Illustration by Celina Hernandez

Illustration by
Stephanie Mided

GET OUTTA HERE, THIS IS MY COMIC!

PLAYER SELECT

Illustration by Sir Gryphon

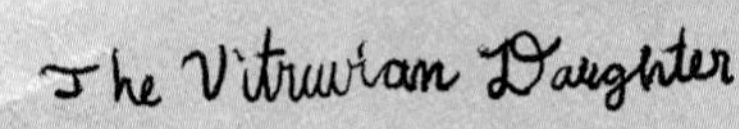

Qualities
- modest
- cool costume
- arms, legs
- no back-talk
- stops time?
- Photogenic

By Leonardo Davincio

Illustration by Crispin Wood

MR. GREAT GUY'S GIRL FRIEND

Illustration by Joshu

tiny eyebrows
The dulcet tones of Linkin Park
could use a shower
burdened with knowledge
This shirt
CAN'T SLEEP CLOWNS WILL EAT ME
HENCH GIRL
The teenage years
CROCS
they're
mfy")
Daniel

CTHULU BURGER

KIDZ LUV LORD CTHULU

$1 OFF your next order*

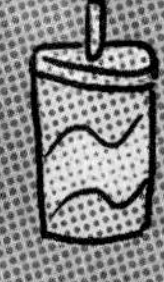